JEWEL OF THE KALAHARI
OKAVANGO

JEWEL OF THE KALAHARI
OKAVANGO

KAREN ROSS

BBC BOOKS

Published by BBC Books
A division of BBC Enterprises Limited
Woodlands, 80 Wood Lane, London W12 0TT
First published 1987

ISBN 0 563 20545 8

Set in $11\frac{1}{2}$ on 13pt Sabon Monophoto and
printed and bound in England by Butler & Tanner Ltd
Frome and London
Colour separations by Technik Ltd, Berkhamsted
Colour printing by William Clowes Ltd, Beccles

CONTENTS

MAPS

For Sands

FOREWORD

Ever since I was first stunned by the wonders of the Okavango Delta in 1973 I have had a strong desire to share its glories with the many people who have neither seen nor heard of it. After a long period I was able to arrange for a two-year-long expedition to produce three films and this book. The basic research was carried out by Karen Ross who also wrote the book.

The area covered was formed where the great Okavango River (the second largest in Southern Africa) hits a fault line and spills out into the Kalahari desert. The waters spread out to form an oasis, the greatest in the world, which supports an astounding web of life.

The book and the film describe the ecology of this amazingly complex system and the way in which life has adapted to both extremes: the harshness of the Kalahari and the jewel-like richness of the great Delta – the Okavango. I believe the films and the book, which were produced at the same time, will complement each other, and I hope that they will help many people to enjoy the wonders of the Delta for many years to come.

Michael Rosenberg, 11 August 1987
Partridge Films, London NW6

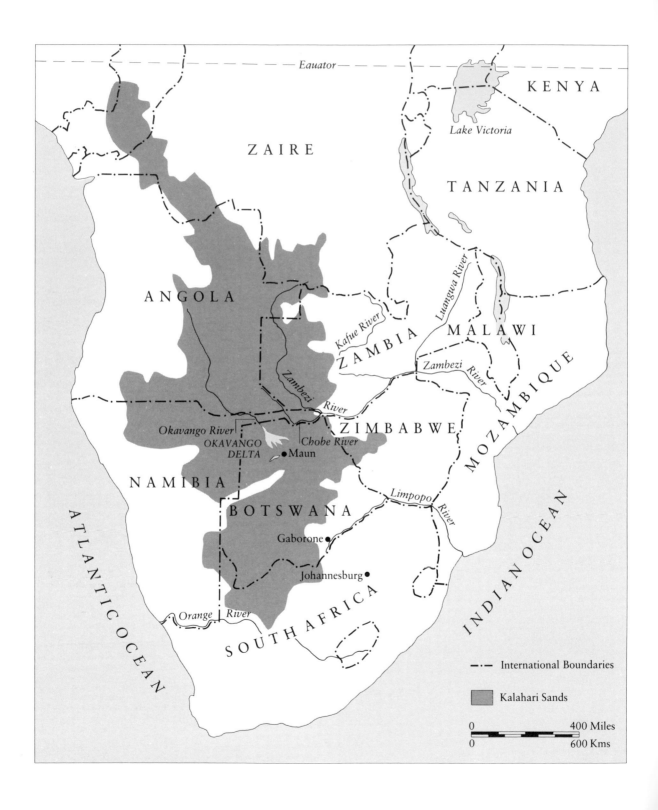

KENYA

ZAIRE

TANZANIA

Lake Victoria

ANGOLA

Kafue River

ZAMBIA

Luangwa River

MALAWI

Zambezi

Zambezi River

River

ZIMBABWE

MOZAMBIQUE

Okavango River

OKAVANGO DELTA

Chobe River

●Maun

NAMIBIA

BOTSWANA

Limpopo River

Gaborone ●

Johannesburg ●

ATLANTIC OCEAN

Orange River

SOUTH AFRICA

INDIAN OCEAN

—·— International Boundaries

Kalahari Sands

| 0 | | 400 Miles |
| 0 | | 600 Kms |

CHAPTER ONE
SANDS OF A CONTINENT

From an eagle's eye view, high in the pale cloudless sky, the land stretches for ever. Awash with browns and yellows, there is no visible water to reflect the eggshell-blue sky and bring a sparkle to the landscape. At this height the wilderness is frighteningly flat, almost dreary; towards the horizon you can see the curve of the earth as it dips beyond view.

The heat from the ground creates thermals which keep the martial eagle soaring, its wings motionless as it circles and searches for food. What life is there in this emptiness? A movement catches the eagle's eye and it swoops lower. On a hot sun-baked mound a small creature screeches its warning. There is a frantic flurry of skinny bodies, long tails and blonde fur as the look-out's fifteen or so companions make a dash for the safety of their communal burrow. Thwarted, the eagle flies off. Catching a thermal, it soars once again over its domain: the Kalahari.

In their burrow, the suricates – a type of mongoose, also called meer-kats – hug each other and twitter and chatter. In a second they are out and foraging again, digging in the sand for scorpions and beetles, only half aware of the danger from the skies because they have a guard to watch for them. The replacement look-out now takes its post on a rise in their otherwise flat territory. Standing on its hind legs the look-out stares at the sky, its distinctive black belly and highwayman mask offering protection from the searing sun. Suricates, together with a handful of 'desert'-adapted mammals, have evolved a unique way of dealing with the harsh life of the Kalahari. They depend on each other for safety, for food, and for help when needed. They are amongst the most sociable creatures on earth.

This is the central Kalahari, in the heart of Southern Africa. Sand dominates the landscape, which stretches for hundreds of miles without surface water except after rain – and here the rain is fickle. Sand is perhaps one of nature's harshest habitats. Like a sponge it sucks and drains any water that touches its surface. Over millennia this gradual seepage of water has taken nutrients with it, leaving a sandy soil deficient in many minerals. The coarse grains make a harsh and gritty medium in which it is difficult to live and move about. Unless stabilised by vegetation, the sand is carried away by the wind. It also reflects the heat of the sun without mercy.

There is, however, a surprising variety and abundance of life here. Often it is in unexpected forms, such as the suricates. The plants and animals have evolved wonderful ways of coping with the heavy heat of summer, the icy cold of winter, and the harsh nature of the Kalahari sand.

Rainfall increases from south to north across the sand face, producing a change in the vegetation. In the south, where the Kalahari is truly arid, ochre-red dunes and wide 'rivers' of sand dominate the landscape. In the central region a slightly higher rainfall supports acacia grasslands, which merge into the deciduous woodlands, rivers and swamps of the north.

Our story is set in the Middle Kalahari, in the northern part of Botswana. This is a transition zone, a land of anomalies, where the sands are covered by the Okavango Delta, an expanse of fresh blue water and floating emerald islands of reeds. Beside the delta are the dry remnants of an ancient lake, adding to the variety of habitats. It is here that the 'desert' displays its most astonishing diversity.

With such variety of landscapes it would seem difficult to define the extent of the Kalahari, but it has two unifying features: its blanket cover of thick sand, and the resulting flatness of the terrain. Geologically, the Kalahari is a huge sand-filled basin in the heart of Southern Africa. It is the largest continuous stretch of sand in the world, covering some 2,500 kilometres from the Orange River of South Africa northwards to the tropical forests of Zaire. During its formation it has undergone some fascinating changes, many of which have only recently been discovered. There is tantalising evidence that it was once a lush area covered by sub-tropical forests, wide rivers and huge lakes.

The origins of the Kalahari go back 135 million years. At this time the southern 'super-continent' of Gondwanaland was beginning to break up, giving birth to Africa as a continent. The reptiles were the dominant animals on earth, having followed the evolution of insects, fish and amphibians. Mammals were tiny nocturnal creatures, hiding from the predatory dinosaurs that roamed the ancient super-continent.

Gondwanaland was destined to form the world's southern continents. It consisted of a series of tectonic plates (huge sections of the earth's crust) which began to drift apart, each carrying its own selection of animal and plant life. India and Madagascar were first to sever their connection; then Antarctica and Australia broke away from the south-east side of Africa. Perhaps a million years later South America moved off westwards. By 100 million years ago Africa stood alone as a continent, much the shape it is today.

Soon after its isolation, much of Africa was uplifted by the inner rumblings of the earth. In the interior of the continent great basins were formed – Chad to the north, the Congo Basin in Central Africa, the Kalahari to the south. Then, for sixty million years, the landscape was relatively peaceful. High areas were gradually worn down by the relentless activity of water, ice, heat and wind, and the basins slowly filled. During this period the Kalahari Basin received the sands of the continent.

Once Africa had become a separate land mass, its movements did not cease. The continent drifted southwards, and its climate became increasingly dry. This resulted in changes to the Kalahari's vegetation, as sub-tropical forests gave way to thorny scrub and plants which evolved remarkable adaptations to aridity. These plants still occur in the Kalahari today. As scrub and grassland took over from forests, so new animals evolved. Since there are no major land barriers in the region, many birds and larger mammals probably migrated from the north and south, creating an even greater diversity of animal life.

The long period of stability and gentle erosion was disrupted by violent activity some thirty million years ago. The giant continent was finally awake; Africa was rocked, buckled and broken. A series of great rifts were formed, stretching from the Red Sea almost 5,000 kilometres along the east of the continent and ending just north of the Kalahari. At these rifts the tectonic plates were drifting apart, in a process similar to that which broke up Gondwanaland. The earth's crust was stretched and thinned, resulting in volcanic activity along the lines of stress. The rifts, volcanoes and uplifts raised the landscape to new heights, restricting the passage of moist air from the north and resulting in even more arid conditions for Southern Africa.

The climate of the Kalahari was made drier still by the glaciation of an ancient neighbour, Antarctica. As this continent moved towards the South Pole and completed its glaciation, about five million years ago, the cold sea currents and air flows which iced over the huge continent sucked up the moisture of the southern atmosphere, bringing drought and dryness to the Kalahari. With the arrival of intense aridity, strong winds spread the Kalahari's sand mantle widely and evenly. It was during this period that plants and animals evolved many of the remarkable adaptations that enable them to withstand long periods of drought.

About three million years ago the climate was at its driest, and the Kalahari was a truly arid place. Strong easterly winds blew the sands into long dunes orientated east to west, running in parallel ridges across the Middle Kalahari. These dunes influenced the flow of rivers during the wetter times that followed, contributing to a remarkable event: the Kalahari's sands were to form one of the largest lakes that Africa has seen, Lake Makgadikgadi. The Okavango Delta of today is the last remnant of this ancient lake.

The sand dunes are now stabilised by vegetation. Depressions between the ridges catch water run-off from the infrequent rains, forming wide winding river valleys which for the most part carry only sand. They are called 'fossil valleys' because they are the remnants of ancient rivers which once carried huge volumes of water across a wetter Kalahari. Even now these old valleys act as drainage channels, and although they are rivers of sand for most of the year, beneath their surface flows subterranean water.

Few plants can tap this deep water source. The appropriately-named camelthorn acacia grows along the banks of the valleys, sending roots thirty metres into the sand to reach water. Occasionally a grove of dead trees indicates a place where the water-table has dropped below the reach of their roots. The subterranean water allows these magnificent trees to spread along the lines of these linear oases, deep into the heart of the Kalahari. With them comes a host of creatures which could not otherwise survive, such as acacia rats, social weaver birds and bushbabies.

Lesser bushbabies are endearing little creatures, with huge eyes, long tails and soft down-like fur. Primitive primates, they spend their lives in trees where they nest in hollows or disused birds' nests. They supplement their staple food of insects with the gum of acacia trees, which becomes an important part of their diet in the dry season. Although lesser bushbabies tend to forage alone they are highly social, with over twenty-five vocal sounds such as grunts, clicks, twitters and chatters. They rest and sleep in their tree hollow in small family groups.

Lesser bushbabies occur mostly in the woodlands of the northern Kalahari, but the camelthorn trees along the fossil river valleys allow them to live in the more arid parts of the Kalahari, too. They are creatures of the night, their huge eyes helping with night vision, and they are able to turn their heads through 180 degrees to compensate for being unable to move their eyeballs within their eye sockets. They moisten their hands with urine, partly to mark their territory and also to help get a purchase as they leap from branch to branch with spectacular bounds, their main way of moving. They have long fingers, adept at grabbing insect prey as it flies past; the insect is then eaten rather like an ice-cream cone.

The camelthorn is an important tree in the arid sandveldt of the central Kalahari. Its leaves, flowers and pods are a valuable food source, while its shady canopy provides shelter from the fierce noonday heat for all manner of creatures, from the desert agama lizard to the Kalahari lion. Plants, too, benefit from the shade. Beneath the leafy canopy grow sweet perennial grasses that are more nutritious than those growing in the surrounding sandveldt. This is partly due to the benefits of a cooler, moister growing place, but is mostly a result of the soil, which is enriched by the nitrogen-fixing microbes in the roots of acacia trees.

The camelthorn flowers and sets fruit just before the rains, when most grasses are dry, so providing alternative food for herbivorous animals. Each year the landscape is graced by its yellow pom-pom flowers and the massed purple blossoms of the rain tree, attracting and feeding pollinating insects. The showy flowers do sometimes signal rain, but often they come and go and the rains do not arrive. Unlike the smaller plants, the flowering of these trees is probably triggered by increasing day-length rather than the promise of rain.

At the onset of the Kalahari summer, which lasts from December to March, the camelthorn produces hundreds of thick half-moon-shaped pods which bear seeds. Unlike most acacias, these pods do not split to scatter the seeds. Instead the tree depends on animals to eat the pods; the seeds are passed out of their digestive tracts unharmed and so dispersed. Indeed larger animals such as giraffe and gemsbok relish the pods as a rich food source. The tree's generous gift of nourishing pods is a way of encouraging the spread of its seeds, particularly in an arid environment where water cannot help in dispersal.

Not all creatures act as harmless seed-dispersers, however. Rodents, in particular, feed on the seeds themselves. The pouched mouse, a slow-moving creature that does not linger long outside its burrow, will gnaw through camelthorn pods and collect the seeds in its cheek pouches. Carrying any other seeds and insects it has collected on its foraging trip, the mouse returns to its burrow to eat its food at leisure and in safety.

The shepherd's tree also provides food, water and shelter in an otherwise harsh land. The food value of its leaves is said to be only slightly less than that of the best livestock fodder, lucerne. Its flowers are rich in honey and the summer berries are eaten by many creatures, from pied babblers to black-backed jackals. In older trees the wizened trunks collect rainwater. These beautifully-adapted desert trees are a lifeline in the Kalahari.

The difficulties of life in sand are compounded by the relentless heat of summer and the unpredictability of rain. In some years heavy rains can transform the parched land into a carpet of green grass interspersed by flushes of jewel-like flowers. But the wet season may be followed by years of drought. Not surprisingly, plants and animals have had to compromise in their adaptations to the arid conditions. Plants need sunshine to grow, but sunshine desiccates. Animals must feed, but they lose water in doing so. Those that survive the Kalahari are those that have found the best compromise.

The central Kalahari is a wilderness of sun-bleached grasses which sparsely cover the endless blanket of sand. In the scorching heat and cloudless skies only the wind whispers and stirs the golden blades. Dotted among the savanna grasses are stunted thorny thickets of the acacia blackthorn, interspersed by shrubs and herbs that blossom only briefly after rain. Their harvest lies buried beneath the sand – succulent roots and underground tubers swollen with moisture. These are the plants that survived as the Kalahari dried under the influence of the Antarctic glaciation. Unable to withstand the increasing dryness and heat, the woodlands receded north-wards and grasses took their place.

Grasses are vital to life in the Kalahari. Leaves and roots provide food and nesting material, and their seeds are eaten by insects, rodents and birds. The grasses have evolved special ways of surviving in this harsh land: they have extensive root systems that spread out to trap any moisture, and by doing so they stabilise sand that would otherwise snake and shift unhindered across the land. Many of the grasses send out short-lived roots during the rains, to maximise the uptake of additional water. Those grasses that survive more than one growing season, the perennials, often have their roots encased in a sheath of sand which is bound by moisture secreted by the plant – this protects the roots from the drying effect of sandy soils. Under good grass cover the subterranean moisture held deep in the sand, between its coarse grains, may last for many months after heavy rain.

Most grasses are annuals, growing quickly and setting seed at the onset of the cold dry season, which lasts from May to August. This fast growth period is an advantage to the plants, since as seeds they can better withstand the long drought. In winter the seeds lie dormant awaiting the fickle rains which will bring new life and growth. The widespread Kalahari grass is an annual killed by winter frost, but its seeds are dispersed by the wind and quickly germinate with the arrival of rain. The abundance of this grass in the region makes it an important fodder, despite the lengths to which it goes to deter grazing animals. Most of the plant is covered by numerous gland-tipped hairs which, when eaten, release a sticky exudate that blisters the mouths of grazers.

Some grass seeds have evolved ingenious methods to ensure their dispersal and germination. Kalahari plume grass produces feathery white seed-heads which increase the efficiency of wind dispersal. They stick and twist themselves into the sand the moment there is sufficient moisture, thus ensuring that they cannot be blown away when ready to germinate. The wind is the agent of dispersal for most seeds, blowing them across the sands until they meet a sand ridge or clump of vegetation where their random scattering is halted, ready for rain. The seeds and grass fragments collected in this way provide food for the smaller sand-dwelling animals such as rodents and insects. To prevent growth after a freak shower, some seeds have chemicals which inhibit germination; only when enough water has washed away the chemical will growth begin.

Many of the Kalahari's tubers and herbs are also annuals, making seeds an abundant and important food source. The cone-headed katydid, an exotic type of grasshopper, has powerful jaws which crack open grass seeds. The desert pygmy mouse, a tiny nocturnal rodent that occurs widely in the Kalahari grasslands, is able to survive without water but is dependent on grasses for food and cover. Grass seeds are its major food source, but it also eats termites which provide necessary moisture. This mouse takes refuge in a shallow burrow in the sand during the day, and builds a ball-shaped nest of soft grass in which to breed.

The bulk of the birds in the central Kalahari are seed-eaters. Few resident species eat seeds exclusively, however, because seeds contain little water. Those which do, including the double banded sandgrouse and the namaqua dove, must drink regularly. This imposes certain restrictions on their distribution, in a land where standing water is rare. The majority of seed-eaters, such as most larks and the social weavers, augment their diet with insects, which allows them to be independent of drinking water.

Among the most striking birds of the Kalahari grasslands are the world's heaviest flying bird, the Kori bustard, and its close relative, the red-crested khoraan. The khoraan performs a spectacular flight display: after calling, it runs a few metres and then flies ten to thirty metres straight upwards, tumbles over with plumage fluffed, and opens its wings just before reaching the ground. These birds supplement their seed diet with insects, and they also feed on the gum of acacias. The diet of successful birds in the arid parts of the Kalahari involves compromise and flexibility.

Many of the smaller plants have overcome the scarcity of water by retaining moisture in their leaves. Mesembryanthemums and aloes have leaves which hold water, principally for use by the plant itself. However, animals also make use of this water store – more than fifty species of animals and birds were recorded visiting a single aloe plant in the Kalahari. Mesembryanthemums, like grasses, have ingenious dispersal mechanisms to ensure their survival through drought. The seed pods are closed in the dry season, and once ripe they are blown across the sand by the wind. Only with the onset of rain will the valves of the pods dissolve; then the seeds are released to germinate. Wild species of cucumber and tsama melons extravagantly encase their yearly production of seeds in succulent, water-filled fruits. These must have a dispersal function since many creatures, ranging from porcupines to brown hyaenas, depend on these fruits for food and water. Once the fruit is eaten the animals carry the seeds away in their stomachs, to be deposited elsewhere.

Some plants have developed large tubers which store water beneath the sand, nourishing the plant in times of drought. The loose structure of sand is a perfect medium for the unhindered growth of these tubers. The morama bulb or gemsbok bean grows to a great size – one was found which weighed 260 kilograms and contained 200 litres of water. The bulbs have a high protein content, and so they are useful as a source of food as well as water.

The grapple-plant has become an important species since a chemical in its tubers may be one of the world's few cures for arthritis. The plant's name comes from its bizarre form of seed dispersal, in which the seed has a gin-trap device that clasps on to the foot of a passing creature.

The animals of the Kalahari have learnt the secrets of this underground feast, which provides food and water even in the driest times. So too have the San (Bushmen) hunter–gatherers, who survive in this inhospitable land by collecting and making use of more than a hundred species of wild plants. In fact more than two hundred species of edible plants have been recorded from the Kalahari. The San people turn to different food sources at different times of the year, but they have their favourites. These include tsama melons, and underground truffles similar to the delicacies that grow in the oak forests of France. The unpredictability of life in the sands has created the need for plants to lay in rich stores of food and water for times of drought, and many creatures benefit from this secret harvest.

Insects, frogs and reptiles are the oldest inhabitants of the Kalahari. They were in the region in its infancy, when Gondwanaland broke up to isolate Africa. They have had time to evolve some of the most fascinating adaptations, both physical and behavioural, which allow them to thrive in even the most arid and sandy conditions. Termites, which play such a vital role in the ecology of the Kalahari, existed then much as now. Fossil termites 100 million years old show no apparent differences in body form from the termites of today; and the termite mound was probably one of the earliest types of organised community on earth.

The nests of the harvester termite are situated deep in the ground, to avoid extremes of temperature and to retain moisture. The home of a vigorous colony may consist of up to twenty nests, usually widely spaced but connected by a complex system of winding tunnels. In the cold winters the annual grasses die off, and as such they are of little nutritive value to grazing animals. However these dead grasses are food for the harvester termites, which in turn provide succulent termite flesh for other creatures at a time when food is scarce. The termites are at the base of a massive food web that extends throughout the Kalahari grasslands. Even larger mammals, like aardvarks and aardwolves, are adapted to hunting them.

In the intense heat of summer the harvester termites are active at night, but during winter, when night-time temperatures can drop below freezing, they forage by day. They have unusual adaptations to their way of life. The workers have well-developed eyes, unlike other termite species, which are blind. Their heads are covered by a horny brown skin which protects them from the sun's glare, differing from the almost translucent skin of the more familiar nocturnal 'fungus termites'.

The only surface evidence of harvester termite colonies are the small holes through which the workers emerge to collect the grasses. On most grassy stretches in the Kalahari, keen eyes soon detect their comings and goings. Indeed, when these insects are busy, hornbills quickly flock to the ground and with casual dexterity toss the succulent termites down their throats, one after the other. Large black pomerine ants emerge from their nest to overpower and carry away solitary termite workers. When their enemies become too numerous the harvesters descend to their subterranean colony, quickly blocking up the holes as they retreat.

These holes lead to narrow branching tunnels interspersed with small cellars, just below the surface, where the termites temporarily store their food. From here wider tunnels lead downwards into the earth, to the 'hives' where the termites live, surrounded by their store of dry grass. In the cool and safety of the hive the coarse dry food of the sandveldt is processed by being eaten, partly digested and then fed to others, and so converted into usable protein.

While larger creatures sink and labour in the deep sands, the lesser creatures of the Kalahari are as at home as ducks in water. With a fascinating array of body designs, skin textures and colour patterns, they run over the sand, dive through it, and generally thrive in this dry, gritty and abrasive medium. One way or another they are able to use sand – to burrow into it to escape the heat and avoid water loss, to hide from an enemy, or to lie in wait for prey.

The larvae of the dragonfly-like antlion insects use their sandy homes to trap small prey, in particular harvester termites. Their small conical pits are a common sight in sandy areas across much of Africa. At the bottom of each pit, buried in the sand, lives the small grub-like antlion larva. When a passing insect disturbs a few grains of sand, the waiting antlion is alerted and quickly tosses sand at the insect with its head, making it slip farther and farther down the steep sides of the sandy pit. Finally it falls to the bottom, where it is grasped firmly by the powerful claws of the antlion and dragged, struggling, beneath the sand. Here the mouthless predator will use its grooved claws to suck out the body juices of its prey.

Some spiders make good use of grains of sand, to help trap their prey. The back-flip spider digs a small hollow in the sandy surface and incorporates sand grains into its web, which disguises the trap. Once the web is constructed, the spider flips over on its back and pulls the web over itself, waiting for its prey to become entangled in the camouflaged snare.

Beetles, especially ground beetles, are the most common insect group in the Kalahari. Many cannot fly since their wing cases are firmly joined, and the wings beneath have long since disappeared. They are generally fierce predators with powerful pincers, obtaining moisture from the body fluids of their prey. They hunt by moving fast on the ground, mostly at night. Fossils from the central Kalahari dated at 95 million years ago (when the Kalahari was slowly filling with sand) show that beetles were the most common insects even then. The group showing some of the finest adaptations to life in sand are the tenebrionid beetles, found in arid regions throughout the world. Many are sand specialists, able to 'swim' through it because of their flattened body shape; they also have remarkable ability to store water.

Carabids are the dominant beetle group in the Kalahari, and most have fascinating methods of chemical defence. Members of the *Anthia* genus are large black beetles with yellow dots and stripes on the body. They are ferocious hunters, catching their prey with powerful pincer-like jaws. As a means of defence they squirt formic acid at potential trouble-makers. The Kalahari sand lizard seems to make good use of the chemical defence mechanism of these beetles, since the juvenile lizards mimic the noxious *Anthia* and so gain a measure of protection. Whereas the adult lizards are yellow and brown with pale orange tails, well camouflaged in the Kalahari sands, the juveniles are strikingly different – black with yellow markings, mimicking the coloration of the beetle. The mimicry extends to movement: the adult sand lizards walk with a normal lizard gait, their bodies undulating from side to side, while the juveniles walk stiff-legged, with arched backs, their reddish tails held flat against the ground in camouflage. In this way both the coloration and locomotion of the young lizards is designed to deceive potential predators into believing they are unpleasant ground beetles. Should the deception fail and the predator pursue, the 'beetle walk' is abandoned and the young lizards dart speedily to cover! As the juveniles grow they take on the adult coloration and abandon their beetle-like locomotion. Surveys have shown that the number of broken tails is much lower in juvenile Kalahari sand lizards than in other closely-related lizards. This suggests their beetle mimicry reduces predatory attacks. For example, Kalahari sand lizards are the favourite prey of secretary birds. However one bird's crop was found to contain fifty-six adult lizards – but not one juvenile.

Reptiles also show superb adaptations to arid environments. They have evolved a reproductive system that is independent of water, and a skin largely resistant to water loss. Many of the Kalahari's lizards are fast-moving ground-dwellers, with long webbed toes and streamlined bodies to help them move speedily over sand. When the surface becomes scorchingly hot these lizards stand on alternate pairs of legs, keeping the other two legs raised and cool in an extraordinary manoeuvre called 'thermal dancing'. Some lizards climb vegetation in order to cool in the wind. The Kalahari spiny agama perches on the branches of acacia trees in the summer. At this time the agama is brightly coloured, so the perching may be a mating display as well as a way of keeping cool. The lizard probably chooses to be in a tree since it is without its normal ground-coloured camouflage.

The Kalahari sands are home to a wide variety of skinks, which during their evolution have become almost legless lizards, enabling them to move through sand effortlessly by 'swimming' through the grains. The snakes, the last of the great reptile groups to evolve, have taken the legless-lizard concept to an elegant extreme. The development of impermeable skins and unusual body shapes are solutions to some of the problems posed by this arid and sandy habitat, but there is still the relentless heat of summer to cope with. A large number of the snakes found in the Kalahari are adapted to living below ground. The blind snakes and worm snakes have adopted this strategy. They are a primitive group, almost as closely related to lizards as they are to true snakes. The short blunt head, covered by a shield and highly polished scales, makes it easier to burrow. They are usually associated with termite mounds, where they take their termite prey. The shield-nosed snake, a beautiful black, coral and sand colour, occurs in sandy areas and spends the day in rodent burrows, emerging at night to hunt. It also has a short head covered by a curved shield, which protects it when burrowing.

One of the best-adapted snakes in the Kalahari is the burrowing adder. Although it resembles the harmless burrowing snakes, it is in fact a deadly predator. Its small head restricts normal striking, so instead it retracts its lower jaw to reveal the flattened fangs, which then strike their prey sideways – an effective way of catching lizards and rodents in small underground passages.

The small mammals of the Kalahari have the same solution to the problems of water conservation and keeping cool – they too burrow. The rodents, perhaps the most numerous of the small mammal groups, excavate burrows deep below the surface where they maintain a cool and humid microclimate. Most species not only dig deep burrows in the sands and dune slopes, but they are also nocturnal in habit, to minimise water loss through heat. The various gerbils are long-legged rodents, a body design followed by similar creatures in the deserts of Australia and North Africa. The bushveldt gerbils live in colonies deep below the sand. The entrance is usually situated beside a clump of vegetation, so the sand is stabilised. Failing that, they may locate their burrows below patches of sand solidified by the urine of larger mammals. These gerbils do not store food like some other small rodents, such as the pouched mouse, but have learnt to supplement a dry diet of seeds with succulent plants. Gerbils play an important role in the Kalahari sandveldt, since their burrowing activities and droppings create a richer soil which plants can colonise. Also their cool moist burrows are, perhaps unwittingly, shared with scorpions, millipedes and beetles.

In a prolonged drought even a burrow can do little to alleviate the harsh reality of heat, no water and little food. In these conditions the various Kalahari creatures resort to different tactics. The larger animals move off in search of food and water, and birds are able to fly away, but the smaller animals – lizards, frogs, tortoises, mice and other rodents – can do neither. So many aestivate until conditions get better.

Aestivation is the arid-land equivalent of hibernation in cold climates; it is equivalent to a long sleep where the body just ticks over, enabling creatures to use little energy while they avoid stressful periods. Amphibians are by nature dependent on water, but some frogs can tolerate arid conditions by this method. The Kalahari burrowing frog is one of the few amphibians to have a life-cycle independent of water, but its permeable amphibian skin restricts it to a subterranean life unless it rains. This frog has adaptations in its tissue fluids that help it retain water, as well as a large bladder that enables it to store and recycle water while it aestivates underground.

Everything about this little frog is fascinating, not least its appearance. Only two or three centimetres long, it has a fat round body, a tiny head and small feet. This is one frog that cannot jump – in fact it is so well adapted to arid conditions that it cannot even swim. During the rains it emerges at night to feed on termites and ants, particularly the flying 'alate' termites that emerge in huge numbers following a heavy downpour. Because of the strange shape of the male, whose fat tummy and short arms make it impossible for him to embrace a female, burrowing frogs have invented a new way of mating. They exude a sticky white substance which acts as a glue, attaching the male firmly to the female as he perches on her back. The glue is necessarily strong, for the pair then dig into the soil with their back legs, and with a slow revolving motion disappear backwards into the earth. The two frogs find a suitably moist spot and excavate a cavity in which the female lays up to thirty eggs (it is still a mystery how the pair becomes unglued). Here the most remarkable event occurs since the whole life-cycle, from egg to tadpole to young frog, is completed within the egg, without the need for external water. Finally the small froglets dig their way out of the nest to the surface. When the breeding season and rains are over they burrow backwards once more, deep into the earth where the sand is permanently moist. Here they wait in suspended animation for the next rain – perhaps a year, perhaps three, or maybe even longer.

CHAPTER TWO

REALM OF
THE UNICORN

The large animals of the Kalahari also exhibit many ingenious behaviours and clever designs that enable them to survive the heat and dryness without standing water. Many of these creatures are outstandingly beautiful. Some are so secretive that they are seldom seen, and man still has much to learn about their behaviour and their way of life. Although water-dependent animals such as zebras and elephants once wandered the grasslands of the central Kalahari, they became extinct there as the increasing aridity dried up the last water pans. Only those creatures that are adapted to survive without drinking water can be considered as true residents of the arid interior. For here there is no standing water except after rain, and rain may not come for many years. As the Kalahari has become increasingly dry over the millennia, droughts are the norm and wet years the exception.

The arid interior is the realm of the gemsbok, a large antelope of the oryx family, whose beauty is matched by its superb adaptations to desert life. Both sexes carry long rapier-sharp horns, whose definition is enhanced by the dramatic black face stripes, and which provide a lethal defence against all predators, even lions. Their glossy silver-grey coats reflect and help dissipate the relentless heat. Gemsboks have perhaps the most remarkable physical adaptations to water conservation of any large herbivorous mammal. They can tolerate temperatures that would kill most other mammals, allowing their body temperature to increase rather than lose precious water by panting and sweating. Gemsboks can survive external temperatures of 45°C because the blood which flows along the arteries to the brain is cooled by travelling past a special network of veins, situated in the nasal passage, which carry cooler blood that takes up excess heat. This has the effect of cooling the arterial blood to around 42°C, which is the maximum the brain can tolerate without being damaged. By moderating their breathing, breathing more deeply rather than more rapidly and thereby minimising water loss, they are able to increase the air flow over these fine nasal veins and so improve cooling.

The importance of gemsboks in the drier regions of the Kalahari is reflected in the folklore of the San people. When a young girl enters womanhood, a gemsbok is killed and she must wear a bonnet made of the antelope's stomach. This is to keep her young and strong, for they say that of all the Kalahari's animals, it is the gemsbok that carries its years the best.

A great array of antelopes and grazing animals evolved as the forests of the Kalahari receded and grasslands took their place, but only a handful have the adaptations to survive without water. Besides the gemsbok, these include the springbok, greater kudu, red hartebeest, and eland. These animals are ruminants, that is, they have an extra stomach where micro-organisms digest plant material with which ordinary stomach acids cannot cope. They also store additional moisture in the rumen for use in times of water shortage. Through careful choice of habitat and flexible feeding behaviour, they are able to survive on plants that provide them with essential moisture as the need arises. Thus each species has a place for itself within the small variations of topography and vegetation which overlay the thick blanket of Kalahari sand. The basic habitats are the sand dunes, the ancient drainage points (fossil valleys, and dry water-holes and lake beds), and the flat sandy plateaux.

The sides of river valleys are lined with sandy banks which rise into sand-dune ridges. The shallow pans (drainage points which form dry lake beds for most of the year) often have a dune on one side, formed by the prevailing wind which scoops up the sand from the pan floor, thus maintaining both pan and dune. Grasses do not grow well in the deep sands of the dunes, but plants that store their food and moisture reserves underground thrive in the loose sandy soils. There are trees such as the camelthorn acacia, the silver terminalia and the leadwood tree, which send their roots deep into the sand to tap the underground water. This means, somewhat surprisingly, that there are sand dunes capped with woodlands of shady trees, overlooking the longer grass and thornveldt of the surrounding plateau and the short grass of the pans and winding dry valleys.

The pans and dry river valleys have a higher clay content than the sands of the dunes and plateaux. Over millennia the water draining into these depressions has carried with it a suspension of clay particles and organic matter, which are deposited on the surface. This slows the drainage of water after rain, temporarily providing animals with areas of standing water. The difference in soil and drainage also has an effect on the vegetation. Because of seasonal waterlogging, trees do not grow on the pan and valley floors. The soils here favour short grasses instead. Surprisingly, these short grasses, even though on the heavier clay soils, dry faster than the vegetation on the arid dunes, due to differences in water-storage capacities between sand and clay. This anomaly further enhances the importance of the dune woodlands to animals in the dry season. Juxtaposed, however, these two habitats offer a wide variety of food plants and cover to animals, which are able to move from one to the other according to the dictates of changing seasons.

The trees, shrubs and underground foods of the sand dunes provide sustenance for browsing animals such as the giraffe and kudu throughout the year. Steenboks, small desert-adapted antelopes with large rabbit-like ears which help dissipate heat, also live in the wooded slopes of the dune crests. They are solitary creatures, living all the year round in well-marked territories which they defend from other members of their species, so protecting their precious food resources, rather than having to move to new grazing areas as many of the Kalahari's antelopes must do. Elands, on the other hand, are highly mobile, ranging over huge areas in their search for food and moisture. They switch their diet from grass to leaves as conditions demand. Red hartebeests and ostriches wander the thornveldt of the plains, digging for plants and browsing on small bushes and grasses. Red hartebeests will form big herds and are migratory – although they are less water-dependent than the other migratory species of the Kalahari, the wildebeest, since they will dig for tubers in the dry season.

Gemsboks and springboks have a daily pattern of movement from one habitat to the other as they seek the shade of the wooded dunes during the day, moving to the open treeless pans and valleys to feed in the cool of late afternoon. In addition, these animals show a marked seasonal movement in response to the changing availability of food and the need for additional moisture.

When the land is green, both gemsboks and springboks generally prefer the short grass and open habitat of the pans and valleys, and they concentrate here after rain. Gemsboks will seek cover in the wooded dunes if they are aware of predators nearby; springboks on the other hand will move to the centre of the open areas if they sense danger. 'Stotting', also called 'pronking', is a method of locomotion the springbok employs when alarmed (though it is not unique to that species, since small antelopes such as oribi and Thompson's gazelle, and even the bat-eared fox, also stot). It consists of a bounding leap, with back arched and all four legs stiff, and a fan of white back-hairs fully erect. The animal lands on all four stiff legs simultaneously and immediately bounces up again, bounding along like a child on a pogo stick. The origin of this peculiar form of locomotion is not clear. It may be a ritualised leap which warns others of danger. It has also been suggested that it is a method of moving which conserves energy, enabling the antelope to look around and pinpoint the predator while still moving away with the minimum of energy output. If an individual is singled out by a predator and the chase begins then the alarmed springbok will try to escape at a full speed, having quickly abandoned the 'stotting' locomotion.

When conditions are dry, however, the pans and valleys are no longer such suitable habitats. Their clay soils are more sensitive to the amount of rain than sandy soils, their grasses drying more quickly than on the dunes and plains. Furthermore there is a greater abundance of roots, tubers and leaves on the dunes, and better shade. In the dry season, therefore, gemsboks disperse over the dune crests to search for tubers and underground food, which they dig with their elegant but powerful and sharp hooves. Springboks also disperse during the dry season although, perhaps because of their less powerful build, they dig less and browse more than gemsboks. Since most Kalahari grasses retain some food value even when dry, this switch in the dry season to browsing the shoots, leaves and flowers of herbs and bushes must be linked to satisfying the animals' moisture requirements. The dry season dispersal in the Kalahari, as the animals spread out to search for scattered and scarce food items, is an unusual feature – a wet season dispersal is more typical, as in the wetter habitats of the north.

Adult male gemsboks are territorial, although they are fairly tolerant of other males in their territories. One advantage of the territory is that the holder has the right to mate with females that might be within his area. The females wander in small mixed groups of a dozen or so individuals, covering an annual range of 100 to 200 square kilometres, which encompasses the territories of many males. These ranges are surprisingly small for the Kalahari when compared to the ranges of the eland, hartebeest or wildebeest. Gemsboks are so well adapted that they need a relatively small area to meet their survival needs, even in severe drought. They benefit from a limited but familiar range where they know how to meet their food and water requirements.

The smaller springboks differ in many ways from the gemsboks, although they too are well adapted to life in the Kalahari. They are gregarious, moving in small herds in dry periods, but forming huge concentrations when local conditions such as rain draw many herds together. Rain may occur in a particular area once in a decade, but springboks have the mobility to reach the place when the rain comes. Their migratory instinct is so strong that once on the move nothing will stop them. Males are capable of mating at all times and the sprouting of green grass is the only environmental trigger or 'cue' which the females need to come into breeding condition. Female springboks can attain this breeding condition at any time during the year, unlike seasonal breeders such as impalas, and so they are able to be opportunistic about the best time to reproduce. They have a short gestation period of twenty-four weeks, and when conditions are favourable they can 'lamb' twice in a year. In optimal conditions the offspring reach puberty in six months (compared to two years in most antelopes), and so populations can quickly build up.

This ability to respond quickly to favourable conditions may be the cause of the remarkable numbers of springboks recorded in the last century. There are legends of their great treks over the arid plains of Cape Province.

Perhaps they moved in search of rain and fresh pastures, or perhaps their numbers had grown so great that there was the universal, undeniable instinct to disperse. Great treks occurred four times in the last century, with estimates of their numbers in any one migration ranging from half a million to 100 million; no one who recorded these events failed to be amazed by the vast numbers. The rinderpest outbreak of 1896, which devastated livestock and wild antelopes alike, no doubt caused the end of these massive migrations. With a vastly reduced population, and large areas of land taken over by the activities of man, those great herds are now reduced to isolated populations in their last domain – the Kalahari.

The pans scattered throughout the Kalahari are an important characteristic of the area. There are many different types – salt pans, rock pans, clay pans – and they vary in size from depressions a few hundred metres across to dry lake beds several kilometres wide. They are an important habitat for animals in the Kalahari, for they are richer in minerals, salts and water than other areas, and they have a marked effect on animal movements. The presence of these mineral-rich pans may explain why the more water-dependent creatures, such as wildebeest, leave the security of the permanent rivers to venture deep into the harsh interior.

The sands of the Kalahari are generally infertile, and particularly low in essential minerals such as phosphorus and nitrogen. Most plants and animals that survive here have adaptations to compensate for this shortage of nutrients. Herbs of the pea family, and some shrubs and trees of the acacia group, are specialised plants that are able to supply their own nitrogen fertiliser. Micro-organisms in their roots extract nitrogen from the atmosphere and make it available to the plant, while also enriching the soils and the grasses growing amongst them. Antelopes obtain additional phosphorus and calcium by chewing the bones of other animals – which is also a common practice amongst Africa's largest rodents, the porcupines. Carnivores obtain these minerals as part of their natural diet.

The low fertility of the Kalahari's sands is partly related to their low clay content, which is usually the 'active' part of the soil as far as fertility is concerned. The grasses growing on the clay soils of pans and valleys are naturally higher in minerals than the plants of the surrounding sandveldt. After rain the pans are covered by a few centimetres of shallow water, which attracts a great variety and number of birds and animals. The water sometimes lasts for a few days, though in deep clay pans it might persist for a month or more if it rains again. Springboks have an astonishing ability to drink water so salty that it is unpalatable and even lethal to most other species. As the water is evaporated by the sun, underground moisture, containing the salts and minerals of the earth, seeps up to replace it. These salts and minerals are deposited on the surface as the last of the moisture evaporates. When the pans are dry they often have well-used digs and earth-licks, where animals have been to obtain the precious salts.

After rain the pans and valleys are the focal point for large concentrations of antelopes, which in turn attract predators. Lions wait in the thick bush on the pan edge or dune slope, ready to hunt the antelopes that are attracted to the salt licks and good-quality forage on the pan and valley floors. In the heat of summer most animals spend the day in the shade of the dune woodlands, moving to the treeless pans at dusk to feed through the night. By grazing at night the antelopes of the Kalahari are able to obtain extra moisture taken up as dew by the leaves of grasses and shrubs. Without a cloud blanket in the sky the heat of the sand is quickly lost at night, and as the temperature drops, the humidity of the air increases rapidly until its dew-point is reached. Plant cells soak up the dew, even in the leaves of frost- or drought-killed grasses. Both plants and animals benefit from this nightly harvest of water.

At dusk, the calls of barking geckos resound over the sandveldt. These are the sharp barks of territorial males, calling from the entrances to their sandy burrows, the shape of which they use for amplification. They announce the night, which belongs to many creatures: they use its dark for cover, and its coolness to conserve water. In the twilight, just before darkness falls, the Kalahari is at its most beautiful and the sandveldt, so barren by day, gradually comes alive with the creatures of the night.

The Kalahari has many unusual predators, most of which hunt and forage at night. They have the typical desert adaptations shown by other creatures: they rest in the heat of day, emerge in the cool of night to search for food, and are flexible in what they eat. Generally the Kalahari carnivores are independent of drinking water. The silver fox, a shy animal, hides during the day in the thick stands of grass on the acacia grasslands, well camouflaged by its silver-grey and gold-flecked fur. At dusk this fox emerges from its daytime hide-out to forage alone, with peaks of activity around sunset and sunrise.

Silver foxes are avid diggers. This is probably how they catch most of their prey, scratching out the sand-dwelling reptiles such as barking geckos as well as their preferred prey of rodents, especially the slow-moving pouched mouse. Like other Kalahari carnivores they are opportunistic feeders, their diet including insects, birds, berries and even some vegetation. The silver fox appears to be less social than its relatives, such as jackals and wild dogs, foraging alone except when the female has a litter of pups.

The black-backed jackal is especially abundant in the arid regions of the Kalahari. While barking geckos announce the summer night, the territorial cry of the jackal is common on winter nights, particularly when the female is on heat. The pair mate for life, rearing their young in disused

aardvark holes. The formation of a strong pair bond has definite advantages, since there is always a mate to help in hunting, scavenging and raising the young. The jackal pair are often helped by the grown-up young of their previous litter, behaviour which is known to improve the survival chances of jackal pups. This shows a greater degree of co-operation within family groups than with silver-backed jackals, which occur only in areas where water is available, and which do not have 'helpers' to assist the pair in feeding their young. It well illustrates the importance of sociability in a harsh climate.

The abundance of termites, ants and other insects in these areas has resulted in the evolution of some fascinating termite specialists. The larger predators of termites are mammals such as bat-eared foxes, aardvarks and aardwolves. They are all relatively large animals, and all pure insect-eaters, even though they look quite different. Because of their similar diet, however, they do have certain characteristics in common, such as weak teeth and jaws, large sticky tongues and acute powers of hearing.

The aardvark is an extraordinary-looking creature, resembling a fat pig with a long snout. A solitary and nocturnal feeder, it has a large range and can cover more than thirty kilometres each night in search of insect prey, principally ants and termites. The aardvark shows several physical adaptations, probably the most important being its long fleshy nose which is very sensitive to smell. As it forages the nose is held close to the ground. Inside the nostrils are numerous fine hairs which help to keep out dust and sand as the creature sniffs for insects. The sensitive snout hairs may be an aid in detecting the movement of insects underground. The thick spade-like claws are strong tools for breaking open rock-hard termite mounds; once in, the aardvark laps up the termites with its long sticky tongue. It is likely that less well-equipped termite eaters such as aardwolves and bat-eared foxes follow aardvarks as they forage.

Aardvarks visit several termite mounds within their territories at regular intervals, returning before the termite's repair on the broken side of the clay mound fully hardens. The powerful claws affect the animal's gait, which is slow and lumbering, making it easy prey for large predators such as lions and spotted hyaenas. Aardvarks dig several different types of burrows: shallow feeding scrapes in the earth or side of termite mounds; temporary burrows with one chamber which are bolt-holes; and permanent burrows with many chambers where a female raises her young. When chased, an aardvark will make a dash for one of the bolt-hole burrows scattered through its territory. If a bolt-hole is out of reach, however, it will dig frantically to create another at a fantastic speed, with showers of dirt shooting out behind. When all else fails and the creature is cornered, it will somersault in a desperate ploy to escape – quite a feat for such a large animal.

Disused aardvark burrows are popular with other creatures who do not have such powerful legs and claws for digging, but who can modify an existing aardvark burrow to suit their needs. So far in the Kalahari seventeen species of mammals, one species of bird and two of reptiles have been recorded using aardvark burrows. Bat-eared foxes will occupy abandoned ones, but they prefer to have their burrows in the firmer soils around the edges of pans. These little foxes are more sociable than the silver fox, and less strictly nocturnal than the aardvark. Although they usually hunt at night, they spend a great deal of time outside their burrows in the day, lying in the sun, playing and grooming. Small and delicately built, they have slim legs and sharp muzzles which offset their huge parabolic ears, used for finding termite prey.

Bat-eared foxes are almost defenceless and are often preyed on by carnivores such as brown hyaenas, as well as by large birds of prey like martial eagles. Probably the only large carnivore against which the bat-eared fox has any chance is the black-backed jackal. If a jackal comes near, an alert fox will arch its back and tail in an alarm signal to others. The foxes may also 'stot' in the same way as springboks, mobbing the irritated jackal while keeping it in constant view. If a jackal approaches a den with cubs, the parents are alerted by high-pitched mobbing barks, and any nearby foxes rush to the den to assist the parents in defending their young.

Bat-eared foxes are highly social, and their large ears and fluffy tails are important forms of visual communication. They pair for life, and live in communal burrows, but they tend to forage alone since they want no distraction or direct competition when searching for their scattered insect prey. However, individuals out foraging maintain contact with each other by soft whistling calls and, on the sudden appearance of a predator, their bushy black-tipped tails are held erect as a rallying signal to others in the group. They cover their feeding areas rapidly, zig-zagging from one spot to another, stopping to put an ear to the ground to listen for subterranean insect activity, and digging rapidly when they locate food. These foxes eat mainly harvester termites, but will also dig up the larvae of tenebrionid beetles and scorpions, sometimes severing the poisonous tails of the scorpions before consuming them. The distribution of harvester termites more or less dictates the distribution of bat-eared foxes, just as the seasonal change in termite activity dictates when the foxes are out foraging. In the winter, when harvester termites are active during the day, so too are the bat-eared foxes – showing a more flexible feeding style than aardvarks, who change their diet to ants in the cold dry season, rather than change their nocturnal habits.

Crude calculations have shown that these various insect-eating creatures consume billions of insects per square kilometre per year. They must, therefore, be important in maintaining some sort of balance in the fragile ecosystems of arid areas. Harvester termites themselves have a major effect on the availability of grass to other grazing animals, since they can remove up to half of the annual grass harvest. In times of drought they are capable of removing the entire grass cover – and have been recorded doing just that on farms where the larger termite predators have been exterminated. It is somewhat ironic that for centuries farmers have killed foxes and aardwolves as carnivorous vermin, when in fact these insect predators probably play an important role in conserving grasslands by controlling the number of termites.

The black-footed cats are late risers, emerging to hunt several hours after sunset. Highly secretive and totally nocturnal, little is known about these fiery felines. They are the smallest of the African wild cats, weighing just over one kilogram. The black-foot is a spitfire of a cat, hissing and snarling at potential danger with green-gold eyes flashing, teeth bared and ears flat against a rounded head. It inhabits the arid grasslands of the Kalahari, preferring open habitats where there is an abundance of rodent prey. During the day, it usually takes refuge in the hollow of a termite mound – hence its nickname of 'anthill tiger'. The black-footed cat is a proficient hunter, preying mainly on rodents such as the pouched mouse or desert pygmy mouse – though in the dry season it adapts, as do other carnivores, to feed on spiders, wind scorpions (or solifugids) and insects.

None of the Kalahari's carnivores has desert adaptations to rival the brown hyaena, a rare animal now thought to be endangered. This hyaena has attractive long brown fur with a tawny-white mantle of longer hair on the shoulders. Such a coat is unexpected in the hot habitat in which the brown hyaena occurs, but is probably necessary in the cold of cloudless night skies – particularly in winter when temperatures drop below freezing. Brown hyaenas have heavy shoulders and powerful jaws typical of the hyaena family, but they are no competition for the more massive and powerful spotted hyaena. Brown hyaenas feed mainly on the kills of other carnivores and they use their broad muzzles and strong jaws to break open the bones, which, together with dry skin, are usually the only remains from a scavenged kill. These shy creatures forage alone at night, relying on their large upstanding ears to pick up the slightest sounds, yet as scavengers they are extremely courageous and steal from large predators with great cunning. They know the movement patterns of leopards and lions, whose range they share, and they find kills by watching the skies for wheeling vultures or listening for the tell-tale cries of jackals.

Relations between the large predators of the Kalahari are never friendly, even if there is no kill to fight over. Every predator is prey to another, although there are definite advantages conferred by size; and even if size protects a predator, there is always the knowledge that their young are vulnerable. Small carnivores such as jackals and bat-eared foxes are preyed on by all the large predators, and brown hyaenas are often killed by lions for they are no match for the 'king of carnivores', and must wait until the lion has moved away from its kill before they feed from the remains. Surprisingly, leopards and cheetahs immediately relinquish their kill to brown hyaenas, for these delicate felines could suffer severe injury from the hyaena's powerful jaws. In the dry season, when only leopards and cheetahs remain in their normal territories, brown hyaenas are top of the scavenging hierarchy and can steal kills from these predators, obtaining fresh meat in the process.

It has recently been discovered that the social behaviour of brown hyaenas is much more complex than previously thought. Their lonely wanderings for food are an adaptation to the harshness of Kalahari life, where food items are scarce and usually widely scattered. Yet they are social creatures, marking grass stems and twigs with a paste from special rectal pouches, which acts as a chemical communication to other brown hyaenas in the area. Each individual mark is a 'calling card' telling others of its identity, social rank and time of passing. The ten or so individuals that share a common range are known to each other; they are in fact members of the same 'clan'. When their paths cross on feeding trips there is an elaborate ritual of greeting, and a strong hierarchy of dominance is evident despite the fact that their meetings are so rare.

The range of a brown hyaena clan covers a territory of about 200 square kilometres, although this increases in times of drought. Each territory includes an area of fossil river valley, so that in the rains there is a short-lived abundance of kills from lions, leopards, cheetahs and wild dogs to feed on. In the dry season the clan enlarges its range to include the woodlands and thornscrub of the dunes and plains, both in keeping with the movements of antelopes and lions, and to search for tubers, fruits and smaller prey such as rodents, insects, birds, termites, spiders and scorpions. This varied menu supplies their only moisture for many months.

During the day the hyaenas lie in the deep shade of acacia or shepherd's trees, waiting for the cool and dark of night before they venture out. When they detect or appropriate a kill they usually hide or 'cache' some of their find in thick grass clumps in the vicinity – particularly when an unexpected abundance of food is discovered, such as a nest of ostrich eggs or a local harvest of tsama melons. There are few other carnivores that 'cache' food, and this is another example of the highly-evolved behavioural adaptations of brown hyaenas to life in this arid wilderness.

A female brown hyaena about to give birth enlarges the hole of an aardvark or bat-eared fox, and in the den she produces her brood of one to four cubs. In the first months she forages alone, but returns to the cubs about

Trees are a lifeline in the sands of the Kalahari. A shepherd's tree in the ochre dunes of the south stabilises the sands and provides food and cover for many creatures.

In the cool of the night the Kalahari comes alive. Bushbabies (opposite) and tree rats (bottom left) remain in the relative safety of thorny acacia trees while a white-faced owl (below) with sharp night vision perches nearby. Bat-eared foxes (bottom right) can detect insect movements with their large ears.

The social ground squirrels (below) live in communal burrows. They keep cool in the day by sand bathing and using their fluffy tails as a shade parasol against the blazing sun. Harvester termites (bottom left), which feed off grass, are eaten by many creatures including spiders (bottom right).

The spiny agama (below left) and sand lizard (below right) obtain moisture by feeding on harvester termites. The burrowing frog (middle right) survives by remaining underground until it rains. The juvenile sand lizard (bottom right) warns off potential predators by mimicking the distasteful *Anthia* beetle (bottom left).

The salty crust of the Pans (below) was formed when Lake
Makgadikgadi's water dried up, creating the largest salt pans in the
world (opposite top). After rain the Pans are covered by shallow sheets
of water (opposite bottom), which will attract thousands of birds
and animals.

Following well-used trails, herds of animals such as zebra (below) congregate to drink at small, rain-filled pans. Lions (bottom) follow in their wake. The wet-season availability of water and food gives lion cubs (opposite) a better chance of survival.

All the Kalahari's animals will drink if water is available – even the desert unicorn, the gemsbok (below), which can survive without drinking if necessary. Giraffes (opposite) have special valves in the blood vessels of their necks so that blood does not rush to the brain when they bend down to drink.

Transformed by rain, the Kalahari grasslands (opposite) are flushed green and studded with colourful flowers. Leopard tortoises (below) emerge from their dry-season retreats, stimulated by the rain to mate. Their protective shell saves them from inquisitive lions (bottom).

The palm belt, stretching north of Ntwetwe Pan, consists of *Hyphaene* palms, which grow in shallow water and were perhaps first brought here by elephants. The palms provide nest sites for birds, and give shade to animals in the open vastness of the Pans.

Opposite: The noisy and gregarious yellow-billed hornbills are common residents throughout the Kalahari region, feeding on insects and seeds and independent of drinking water.

49

twice a night to suckle them. She may move to another den if the flea population gets out of control! When the cubs are three or four months old, a remarkable event occurs. The mother picks them up one by one and carries them to a large den within the territory, which is also home to all other cubs of females in that particular clan. It is the communal 'nursery den'. The young cubs spend the rest of their childhood here, living with the other youngsters, while the females share in procuring their food. These cubs are generally all related, since females born into a clan remain there. Only the males disperse, sometimes covering distances of 600 kilometres. Usually only one female in a clan gives birth each year, which puts a limit on the number of young in the communal den.

Every female of the hyaena clan brings some food to the den from time to time, even if she has had no young that year. Some males also bring food to this nursery, and a nursing female will feed other cubs apart from her own. In this way the group co-operates to feed the hungry youngsters, since several females out foraging are more effective than one lone mother who cannot leave her young for long. Every adult hyaena visiting the den is greeted by a flurry of hungry and excited cubs of all ages and sizes.

The communal den is a remarkable adaptation to coping with the harshness of the central Kalahari. Just as suricates (meerkats) are highly social, feeding and detecting predators as one group, so brown hyaenas co-operate in the raising of their young, even though they feed alone. The cubs are left unattended for much of the time, so they must be constantly alert for the sound of an approaching predator. When alarmed they dive for the safety of the den, their only protection. Inside is a large underground chamber and many small bolt-holes dug by the cubs themselves. Here they are quite safe from marauding lions and leopards. The young remain in the den constantly until they are about eighteen months old, when they leave for the first time under the guidance of a visiting adult. After a few more months they have enough experience of their range to begin foraging alone.

In the desolate Kalahari, where food can be very scarce, and where the solitary foraging of a mother may result in her death by a large predator, the communal den has another advantage: it offers hope of survival to orphaned cubs, which are often adopted by other females. Indeed, it is estimated that seventy per cent of brown hyaena cubs in the central Kalahari are adopted or orphans.

Lions are generally nocturnal hunters, but never more strongly so than in the Kalahari. There is a distinct survival advantage to hunting in the cool of night, when water loss is smaller than during the day and there is more prey about. Lions are the only members of the cat family that are distinctly social, living and hunting in prides. However, their social system is less stable in arid habitats, where the prides seem to break down in the dry season. Although adult lions have adapted their social behaviour to cope with the dryness of the Kalahari, conditions are particularly hard for lion cubs, and juvenile mortality is very high. The communal den system of brown hyaenas shows the advantages that an arid-land specialist has over a carnivore that is flexible rather than superbly adapted to a specific habitat. Sometimes a hungry lioness has to abandon her cubs for several days while she goes out hunting, and she may return to find that they have fallen prey to another predator, or even that they have died of thirst or starvation.

Lions hunt giraffes, kudus and gemsboks in the dune woodlands and the valleys. As their prey scatter, increasingly during the dry season the lions turn to much smaller prey, such as rodents, porcupines, birds, springhares and bat-eared foxes. In the Kalahari, fifty per cent of lion kills are small creatures, compared to only one per cent for the Serengeti lions. In the dry season, or in times of drought, the lion pride disintegrates. Their range may expand some 500 per cent from a few hundred square kilometres to 1,500 square kilometres or more. Individuals wander alone much more and females may be alone with their cubs for many months, mixing with any strangers they might meet. In fact lionesses change prides and pride areas frequently during the dry season. Females mate with strange males, or nurse strange cubs, and males may even feed strange cubs. In other words, the typically strict social organisation of the lion pride breaks down in times of drought – yet another adaptation to life in the Kalahari.

In the depths of the long dry season, dawn brings yet another day of scorching heat and no rain. The pans are dry, the larger desert antelopes have dispersed, and with them their predators. Only a few highly-adapted creatures remain and eke out a precarious existence in an unforgiving land. Waiting for the rain ...

CHAPTER THREE
LAND OF SUN, WIND AND MOON

In the heart of a huge dry lake bed the blazing sun beats down on the white-hot land surface. All around is a snow-like whiteness that blinds and dazzles. The heat is a physical force. There is no horizon; somewhere the land meets the pale cloudless sky – or does it . . .? Mirages give the impression of water, when there is none for hundreds of kilometres. There is no sense of time or place. It is like being in a huge and hot vacuum.

The wind announces the end of the day. With no barrier to slow it down, it screams along the hot ground, occasionally losing control and spiralling upwards in a twisting tornado. The sun sinks slowly, a fireball that colours the land orange, while on the other side of the sky the full moon rises.

When darkness falls the landscape is once more transformed. The moon bathes the ground in a silver light that picks out the faint rise and fall of a low, crescent-shaped sand dune. The horizon is clear now. Perfectly straight, it cuts the spherical world in half as the equator halves the Earth. The star-filled sky forms the upper part of the sphere and the silver-white land is the lower. The only sound is of the wind.

This is the Makgadikgadi Pan, itself composed chiefly of two major pans – Ntwetwe and Sua. It is a vast and ancient inland drainage basin of the Middle Kalahari. Geologists have discovered prehistoric shorelines which marked the fluctuating perimeter of a lake; for it is believed that this enormous depression was once the site of Lake Makgadikgadi, one of the largest ever in Africa. The crusty white surface is composed of saline deposits left behind as the lake's waters were burnt off by the thirsty sun. Covering an area of 37,000 square kilometres, the Makgadikgadi is the largest area of salt pans in the world. What are the secrets of this harsh white land? How did a lake of such size come to be here, in the notoriously waterless Kalahari sands? Where did the water come from, and where did it all go? The Makgadikgadi Pan is still a mystery, but man has at last begun to unearth the fascinating story of its origins.

The drying of the Kalahari, which reached a climax some three million years ago, was followed by a period of much higher rainfall. As the climate became wetter the great rivers of the Middle Kalahari (the Okavango, Chobe

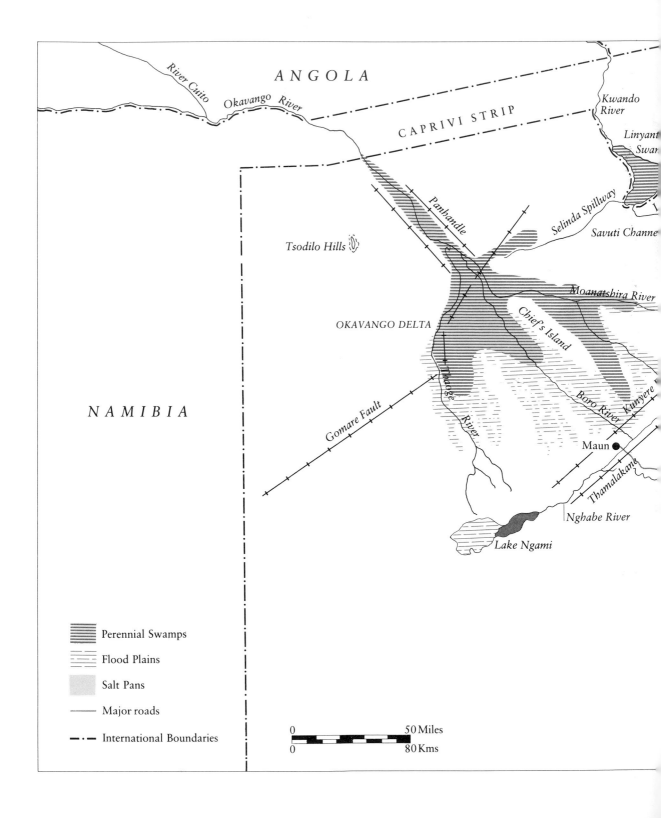

ANGOLA

River Cuito

Okavango River

CAPRIVI STRIP

Kwando River

Linyant Swan

Panhandle

Selinda Spillway

Savuti Channe

Tsodilo Hills

Moanatshira River

OKAVANGO DELTA

Chief's Island

Thaoge River

Boro River

Kunyere

Maun

Gomare Fault

NAMIBIA

Thamalakane

Nghabe River

Lake Ngami

Perennial Swamps

Flood Plains

Salt Pans

Major roads

International Boundaries

| 0 | 50 Miles |
| 0 | 80 Kms |

ZAMBIA

Chobe River

Victoria Falls

Zambezi River

vuti Marsh

Mababe
Depression

ZIMBABWE

Nxai Pan

Nata River

i River

Ntwetwe Pan

MAKGADIKGADI PANS

Francistown ●

Sua Pan

Lake Xau ● Orapa

BOTSWANA

and Zambezi) flowed once more, running south-eastwards via the Limpopo into the Indian Ocean. About two million years ago an upwarping of the earth's crust created a steep valley or fault, called the Kalahari–Zimbabwe Axis. The fault interrupted the flow of these huge rivers into the Limpopo, and thence into the Indian Ocean, causing them to pond back and gradually fill the immense basin of Makgadikgadi. The size of the resulting lake fluctuated with the prevailing climatic conditions of the time. To an experienced eye the different shorelines can still be seen around the perimeters of the pans. It is hard to believe that this harsh and waterless place was ever a lake, with deep fresh waters teeming with fish, birds and crocodiles – a place where early man fished and hunted.

It is thought that at its maximum size, around 60,000 square kilometres, Lake Makgadikgadi included large areas of what is now the Okavango Delta. The lake would have had an hour-glass shape, with the Okavango depression as one part and the larger Makgadikgadi depression as the other, connected by a narrow waist through which the Boteti river valley now runs. At this time, some 20,000 years ago, the drainage basin was probably full to capacity so the waters spilled northwards, flowing into the Middle Zambezi. From here they pushed eastwards to the ocean, forming the Victoria Falls in the process and linking the Upper and Middle Zambezis into one large river.

The seaward release of this large quantity of water no doubt partly drained Lake Makgadikgadi, but other factors were involved in its gradual desiccation. The climate became drier once more, with higher temperatures, causing the rivers to carry less water and the lake to shrink by evaporation. By 10,000 years ago the drying of the Kalahari was well advanced. During this time the sediments carried by the Okavango River were increasingly deposited in Lake Okavango, together with wind-blown sands from the shrinking shorelines of the lakes. Eventually the sands and sediments formed the raised cone-shaped fan which characterises the Delta today.

The formation of a series of faults, including the Thalamakane Fault which isolated the Okavango from the Makgadikgadi, also helped to reduce the amount of water flowing into the lake. As Lake Makgadikgadi continued to shrink the area must have become a series of smaller lakes, which have since fluctuated in size and eventually disappeared. In addition to the two biggest pans of the Makgadikgadi (Sua and Ntwetwe) there are many smaller ones: Nxai, Kudiakau, and the drying remnants of the recent lakes Ngami, Mababe and Xau. All that remains of the water now is the Okavango Delta.

As the great lake slowly shrank, grasslands formed where there was once water. As the lake fragments grew smaller and smaller through evaporation, so the salts within them became increasingly concentrated. Finally the sun burned off the last shallow remnants of water, leaving behind a brittle crust of white salts at the lowest points. These are the pans proper. In them, in the dazzling heat and burning alkalinity, nothing will grow. Here and there a crescent-shaped island of sand, perhaps sculpted by the water currents of the former lake, rises high enough above the salts to permit the growth of spiky grass and the occasional stunted acacia. Large areas of short grasses stretch around the pans, penetrating into them in long ridges and islets that are composed of sands and thus support some vegetation. In retaliation the alkalinity of the surrounding pans permeates the sandy ridges, so that only the hardiest grasses grow there. A specialised lizard, the Makgadikgadi spiny agama, lives under the salt bushes on the edges of the pans. It feeds on tenebrionid beetles and harvester termites, climbing up on grass clumps to cool in the wind and burying itself in the sand to hide from predators.

No animals live on the arid salt pans, although criss-crossing tracks can be seen meandering across them as creatures move from one grass-covered island to another. Occasionally ostriches wander across the pans, large birds that are dwarfed in the emptiness. The ostrich is able to withstand intense heat and to live with hardly any water – two essential requirements for survival in this area. This bird has nasal salt glands through which it excretes excess salts from its body with no wasteful loss of water. It cools itself by fluffing up its back feathers, so protecting its body not only from the heat that beats down from the sun, but also from the heat reflected and radiated up from the white surface of the salt pans. Ostriches also fan themselves with their large wings, sometimes drooping them loosely down by their sides.

The ostrich is the largest bird in the world. Flightless, its success is remarkable in a land full of danger and predators. Birds such as the dodo in Mauritius and the kiwi in New Zealand lost the power of flight presumably because there was no danger from predators – that is, until the arrival of man, himself a predator, who also brought the domestic cat that hunted young chicks. This sudden influx of predators resulted in the extinction of the dodo and the endangering of the kiwi. In Africa, where the list of large predators is formidable, one wonders how the ostrich has survived so well.

Recent fossil finds show that ostriches probably evolved in Europe some fifty million years ago. Already flightless, the birds migrated southwards, perhaps pushed by the advancing Ice Age, walking some 10,000 kilometres until they reached the southernmost part of their natural range in Southern Africa. No doubt the size of the bird, which is perhaps the reason it cannot fly, provides a clue to its great success on the African continent. Its immensely long legs enable it to out-run most predators, while the sharp claws and powerful kick allow an adult bird to protect itself from even a lion attack.

Ostriches have evolved an elaborate social organisation which presumably contributes to the survival of chicks, and so of the species, for the young are naturally the most vulnerable. The habit of adult birds is to nest communally, several females laying their eggs in one nest, although this nest is only incubated by a territorial male and his 'major' hen. The evolution of this behaviour has long been a puzzle which now seems to have been solved. The conspicuous black and white plumage of the males makes them more vulnerable to predators. This means there are more females than males in a population. In addition, the ostrich egg is smaller in relation to the adult bird's size than the eggs of most other birds. So although a female may lay only six or seven eggs, she can incubate three times that number. It therefore makes sense for the 'major' hen to incubate the eggs of other, 'minor' females who do not have their own mate and nest.

But why should only the male and the major hen incubate the eggs – the male at night and the female by day, for six long and dangerous weeks – when half the clutch belongs to other females? We now know that the major female can recognise her own eggs, which she pushes to the centre of the nest. Eggs are preyed on by many creatures, such as jackals, lions and Egyptian vultures to name but a few. However, by her system of incubation the major hen actually enhances the chances of her own eggs surviving by 'dilution', since the outer eggs of the minor hens are more likely to be taken first.

Not only do the pair incubate the eggs, they also take care of the chicks. Often huge 'crèches' form as they take over young birds from nearby nesting pairs. 'Crèches' of over a hundred young ostriches have been seen at the Makgadikgadi Pan. Again this behaviour increases the chances of survival of at least some chicks, by 'diluting' the effects of predation.

Sweeping around the north-west of the largest of Makgadikgadi's pans, Ntwetwe, is a spectacularly beautiful habitat – the palm belt. It seems a fascinating anomaly that groves of palm trees should be scattered among the short grasslands of this arid wilderness. Sometimes the trees lead right down to the white sands and salts on the fringes of the pans. As the fan-shaped fronds rustle and stir in the wind there is an evocative feeling, perhaps the sound of waves on the sandy shore of the lake that was. Since there are few other trees in this grassland belt around the salty pans, the presence of the *Hyphaene* palms poses the question of how they are able to survive. In fact these trees grow well in areas with a shallow, slightly saline water-table which few other trees can tolerate; hence they dominate the vegetation around the pans. Their large ginger-coloured fruits are eaten by many creatures, but only elephants are large enough to be agents for the long-distance dispersal of the seeds they contain. No elephants range as far as the Makgadikgadi Pan today, since the supply of water is too unreliable. Yet the presence of these groves of palms suggests that elephants were once here in large numbers, perhaps when there was a lake, or at least remnants of permanent water. They probably brought the seeds in their stomachs from the Okavango Delta and the great rivers of the north.

Since the palms stand as the only elevation in the grasslands, they provide the only suitable roosting and nesting sites for birds in this region. Vultures nest on the very tops of the palm trees, in large constructions made of sticks and twigs. Often they are associated with red-necked falcons, which nest lower down and lay their eggs in the hollow formed where a frond joins the slender grey stem of the palm. Most of this falcon's prey is caught on the wing and no doubt includes other residents of the palm tree's crown, such as bats and the slender long-winged palm swift. Specialised inhabitants of *Hyphaene* palms, the swifts roost beneath the fronds at night, clinging to their underside. When breeding they build a cup-shaped nest of saliva, feathers and mud, glued to the midrib of the underside of the palm frond, and often with the blade of the frond drawn down around it as camouflage. The eggs are even glued to the lower lip of the nest.

During the dry season the pans are entirely waterless. The salt crust of the ancient lake bed cracks from the shrinking mud beneath, and around its edges the grasses are baked a brittle brown. Few animals can survive in the area throughout the year. Those that can have specialised feeding strategies to enable them to obtain water in this thirst-land. Springboks are one of the few antelopes resident in the palm grasslands fringing the pans, preferring the open habitat where they can detect predators from afar. They obtain moisture by feeding on succulent plants, by browsing on bushes and by digging for underground tubers. Cheetahs are their main predators, and the vast open stretches of grassland around the pans offer perhaps the best hunting grounds in the Kalahari for these magnificent sprinters. Like other predators of arid environments, the cheetah obtains moisture from the blood of its prey, and will also feed on succulent fruits such as the tsama melon. It is generally believed that cheetahs are daylight hunters but in the Kalahari they hunt at dawn and dusk, to avoid heat stress and unnecessary water loss. They also hunt at night in order to catch their second most abundant prey, the nocturnal springhare.

The springhare is a large rodent unique to Africa. With a shaggy ginger coat, long and powerful hind legs, large ears and eyes, and a fluffy tail, it looks like a mixture of a rabbit, 'Bambi' and a small kangaroo. The dry Kalahari grasslands seem an unlikely place for such a creature. Springhares are powerful and fast diggers, living in burrows excavated from the soft sands and only emerging at night to feed. They have a great preference for the short grasses that grow on the very edges of the salt pans, for these are higher in minerals and protein and they are not too tall, which makes predator detection easier. They do not forage far from their burrows, dashing back to escape from predators. A springhare moves on its kangaroo-like hind legs, using its short front legs to feed as it plucks and eats the succulent grass bases and also chews on the spongy outer flesh of *Hyphaene* palm fruits. On moonlit nights the shadows of the palm trees provide the hares with a certain amount of cover. Like many nocturnal creatures they are not highly social, but feed in groups for safety. The abundance of these large rodents in a harsh land makes them an important source of food for all carnivores, including man.

Disused springhare burrows are taken over by many other creatures, from bat-eared foxes, silver foxes and mongooses to snakes and rodents. There are other burrows, apart from those of springhares, scattered among the sandy grasslands, since remaining underground is the best strategy to avoid the intense heat of summer, when ground temperatures in the open rise to over 60°C. Small openings in the sand are evidence of the homes of scorpions, abundant creatures here, and able to withstand some of the highest temperatures of any creature on earth. The disused burrows of rodents, bat-eared foxes and aardvarks provide humid retreats for many lesser creatures including insects, snakes and lizards. Each burrow no doubt has a fascinating sequence of ownership as one species leaves and another takes over.

Aardwolves are mysterious creatures, seldom seen even though they are quite abundant in the arid grasslands around the Makgadikgadi Pan. Their common name is from the Afrikaans meaning 'Earth Wolf', since this slender relative of the hyaena lives much of its life underground. The high shoulders and sloping back of the aardwolf give it a typical hyaena shape, but it is a quarter of the size and weight of even the small brown hyaena. Highly specialised animals, they live exclusively on insects. Evolution has shaped their dentition so well to this diet that their weak jaws and poorly-developed cheek teeth are not strong enough to capture or chew a more fleshy meal. This and their relatively small size make aardwolves particularly vulnerable to larger predators such as lions, leopards and hyaenas, and this may partly explain the importance of burrows to them. Although they often use the abandoned burrows of springhares and aardvarks, they are capable of digging their own dens, especially in the softer sands around the edges of the pans. Some of these are dens for resting in during the day or raising their young. Other, deeper burrows are scattered throughout their feeding range, and are bolt-holes down which the aardwolves can escape should a predator loom too close while they are out foraging.

The nocturnal aardwolf's senses of smell and hearing are highly developed. The large ears, similar in shape and size to those of the bat-eared fox, are no doubt important in detecting and locating the scurrying activity of insect prey, which is then lapped up with a broad and sticky tongue. The aardwolf feeds almost exclusively on termites, although the particular species taken depends on the seasonal activity of the termites. In winter the harvester termite forages during the day, so the nocturnal aardwolves switch their attention to the snouted termites, which continue to be active at night.

To the shy, solitary and nocturnal aardwolves, the sense of smell plays a major role in everyday life. They are prolific scent markers and, like hyaenas, are equipped with anal scent glands with which they can mark or 'paste' an object with a sticky and musky secretion. Aardwolves have different types of marking behaviour which seem to fulfil different functions. They will mark important areas in their territory or range, such as their den, by leaving several large blobs of secretion on a nearby grass stem or twig. They also leave a minute amount of secretion on a grass stem in the area in which they are feeding, perhaps to indicate that the area has been visited that same night, and is therefore depleted of food.

Beyond the palm belt the grasslands of the Makgadikgadi merge into acacia woodland dominated by the spiky bushes of blackthorn acacia, occasionally interspersed with small islands of taller acacia trees which provide shade during the intense midday heat. Despite the inhospitable appearance of the acacia thickets they are a valuable food source for browsing animals such as kudus and giraffes, as well as a dry-season alternative to grasses for springboks and gemsboks. Acacia leaves are much higher in protein than most other leaves in the grasslands, and these trees replenish their leaves as soon as the latter die, so a tree will usually have leaves even in driest times. The acacia's seed pods and flowers are an additional bonus. The seeds of the blackthorn acacia have twice the protein content of even the most nutritious grasses.

The bushy thickets of blackthorn acacia make safe, albeit low, nest sites for secretary birds which breed during the summer months, around the time of the rains. The adult birds stalk pedantically through the long grass, black head quills shaking with each deliberate stride of their long legs. Eagle-sharp eyes and a powerful curved beak are a deadly combination for catching their reptilian prey. They fearlessly kill poisonous snakes such as the slow-moving but quick-striking and deadly puff adder. The bird repeatedly bats the striking snake with the leading edges of its wings, until the snake is exhausted, and then it moves in for the kill – a few lethal stamps from its strong legs. Although renowned hunters of large snakes, secretary birds usually seek smaller prey in order to feed their chicks. The most abundant food source in the acacia grasslands around the pans is the Kalahari sand lizard.

Both male and female secretary birds care for the chicks, returning alternately at two-hourly intervals to feed them after foraging in the grass-lands. Food caught by the adults is stored in the crop and later regurgitated to the begging chicks. Often the parents carry water in the crop too, since the thirsty chicks are exposed to relentless heat in their shadeless nest. On each visit the parents also carry nesting material in their beaks, to re-line and maintain the large nest. When the chicks are nearly fledged they begin exercising themselves by standing on the nest and flapping their wings. To encourage them to leave their home the parents begin to regurgitate food at the base of the nest.

Dwarfing the acacias and palms, a few massive baobab trees exist on the arid edges of the pans – although these African giants are themselves dwarfed by the white vastness of the pans. Baobabs live to a great age and some may be over three thousand years old – perhaps the very same trees that stood on the edge of the great Lake Makgadikgadi. Each swollen trunk may hold up to 9,000 litres of water, which enables the tree to survive the long periods of unreliable rainfall. The extraordinary baobabs have their own world associated with them, providing food, cover and water in a harsh environment. The old trees have hollows carved in them, perhaps by primitive peoples who sought refuge inside the mighty trunks or extracted water from the fibrous wood-pulp. Within these hollows are many unexpected forms of life.

At dusk the ghostly white form of a barn owl perches at the entrance to a large baobab. Making a screeching call it sets off, gliding and hovering over the grasslands beyond the grove of baobabs and the empty salt pan. The male barn owl is out hunting, searching for food to feed his hungry mate who broods their eggs. His favourite prey here is the bushveldt gerbil, which lives in colonies in burrows amongst the grasses, feeding on grass seeds and shoots. When rodents become scarce the barn owl feeds on bats, scorpions, skinks, agama lizards, beetles and termites – the winter diet of this arid environment.

In the huge hollow of the baobab there is often more than one breeding pair of barn owls. They use the same roost and nest sites year after year. The pair bond between the male and female is strong, and they will probably spend most of the year roosting together even when their young have fledged (left the nest). The eggs hatch after a month, but the chicks (as many as eight if food is plentiful) are featherless and undeveloped, huddling together for warmth and physical support in those first weeks. It is only in their eighth week that the young first leave the nest, but they probably remain in the vicinity for much longer. The baobab hollow must be one of the safest places in the exposed habitat of the pan for barn owls to breed.

Despite the dryness, the grasslands are covered by a waving blanket of golden stems. The grazing animals have dispersed in their search for more succulent vegetation, while the water-dependent creatures have migrated to areas of permanent water to the west and the north. The grasses are thus rested. It is this pattern of animal mobility, giving the grasses a rest season, which enables such a remarkable growth of grassland in the otherwise harsh and difficult Kalahari habitat. The balance, however, is fragile. Perhaps if water was brought here all year round the grasses would die back, be over-grazed and uprooted, and the temporarily stable sands would be let loose once more on their crazy wanderings, driven by the wind.

After a long year with no water, the build-up to rain is dramatic. The first sign is an intense and heavy heat. There is a deathly quiet and no movement. Most animals are in their burrows, or resting in whatever shade they can find. Heat waves distort the air, and mirages give the impression of water shimmering over the ancient lake bed. Then the wind picks up with a sudden violence. Whirlwinds and dust devils rise into the blackening sky, carrying hot air and dust as they lean crazily forwards and speed across the pans. Rainstorms fall locally, filling shallow pans with water and attracting large herds of springboks to the new flush of green grass. Rain that falls throughout this immense catchment area gradually drains towards the Mak-gadikgadi Pan. Rivulets run into narrow channels; these flow into the sandy stream beds; dry river beds are briefly flushed with water; and small pans fill up. Although the rainstorms are scattered and brief, the Makgadikgadi basin soon begins to fill with a sheet of shallow water that stretches to the horizon.

The pans are transformed by the simple event of rain. Scattered among the emerald carpet of newly-sprouted grasses are the colourful flowers of desert succulents – mesembryanthemums, aloes and melons, which must complete their life-cycle quickly before the dryness arrives again. Leopard tortoises, which have been in semi-hibernation during the dry winter and the hot months before the rains, now emerge from their retreats beneath logs or just under the soil surface. They feed greedily on the new succulent vegetation from which they obtain their moisture requirements. As with many creatures, the arrival of the rains is a stimulus for the tortoises to mate. The male, who is much smaller than the female, probably locates a receptive partner by scent. Before mating he pushes her until she is in a suitable position. Mating can take hours or even days, and is a very vocal affair! The female lays her eggs in the ground, and the following year the young soft-shelled tortoises will emerge with the rains, ready to feed on the new vegetation. The hard shell of the adult tortoise makes it difficult to kill, and lions will play with one for hours but are unlikely to be able to finish it off. However the young tortoises have softer shells and are preyed on by many carnivores, including eagles which carry the young into the air and drop them to break open the shell.

In the saline waters of the smaller pans there is an unexpected burst of new life. The salty depressions abound with frogs and tadpoles, which feed on aquatic insects and which are in turn hunted by small terrapins, semi-aquatic relatives of the tortoise. Helmeted terrapins occur throughout Africa in shallow and temporary water bodies such as the pans. They can remain buried deep beneath the sand for months, maybe even years. Their large and relatively powerful claws provide useful service, since digging into hard earth is important to their survival. Having spent the dry period in aestivation, they emerge as soon as the pans hold water again. They are active on land and can often be seen basking in the sun, but they are most at home in the water, where they are fast and agile swimmers. These avid hunters wait in ambush for a passing tadpole or frog which has also emerged with the wet. The female digs into earth away from the water in order to lay her eggs in a round chamber some fifteen centimetres into the ground. Since the sun-baked ground is extraordinarily hard, she must soften the spot by discharging her cloacal (body) water onto it. As the pans dry out the adult terrapins dig themselves deep into the earth again, where they remain until the next rain.

The sudden availability of water opens the grasslands to other more water-dependent animals. Zebras and wildebeests abandon their retreats of permanent water and follow the rains. They arrive at Makgadikgadi in their thousands. Scattered throughout the palm belt, they feed on the new grasses, taking advantage of the higher mineral content of vegetation growing near the salt pans and the availability of mineral licks. The grasses are short but relatively abundant, having been rested for the previous year, when the only large herbivores feeding on them were scattered groups of springboks.

There is a minimum of social organisation in the migratory herds of wildebeest, due to the large numbers of animals grouped together. The females follow the good grazing, and the males follow the females, forming temporary territories as they move. A termite mound often forms a central focus, where male wildebeests attempt to collect potential mates. Their low grunting as they call to passing groups becomes a chorus-like mantra when hundreds of animals are on the move. Males frequently fight, fiercely clashing horns and sparring on their knees. The most comic and characteristic of the displays is the 'cavorting' of the wildebeests, as the males leap and bound in displays to one another. So absorbed are they in this territorial behaviour that they are the group of wildebeest most commonly preyed on by lions, many of which follow the seasonal migration.

By the time the wildebeests arrive at the pans during the rains, many have their calves. There is a remarkable synchrony in calving, though probably not as high as in the Serengeti of Tanzania, where eighty per cent of wildebeest calves are born within three weeks. As with ostrich crèches, this abundance of young has the effect of 'diluting' or 'swamping' predation, for there are only so many predators in one place at one time, and they can only make so many kills.

The arrival of so many large grazing animals, and the predators they attract, transforms the empty grasslands. Nomadic lions wait for the cool and cover of darkness before they set out to hunt; for a short time there is an abundance of easy prey in the Kalahari. Despite the presence of water the daytime temperatures are still high, and most animals feed only in the early morning, evening and at night. In the stillness of the noonday heat there is no sound except for the shrill call of the black khoraan as it parachutes out of the sky in a bizarre mating display. As the sun slides to the west the wind picks up and begins to cool the scorching day. Herds of wildebeests, zebras and springboks stir from their resting places beneath the palm groves. As they trek across the grasslands the wind whips up the sand kicked loose by their hooves; soon the landscape is filled with regiments of dark moving shapes, dust flying at their heels, dwarfed by the lines of palms which mark the boundary between earth and sky. A pool of water, coloured deeper blue than the sky, sparkles unexpectedly in the dusty plains. It is towards this that the lines of animals are slowly moving.

There is an air of nervous excitement as the herds walk towards the water pan. They are no doubt instinctively aware of their vulnerability to predators as they drop their guard and lower their heads to drink. Always the wildebeests lead the advancing lines of animals, while zebra stallions canter around the periphery, controlling their harems with high-pitched barking calls. The wildebeests at the head of the line might nervously turn back, and so may the next few, until at last one wades belly-deep into the water to drink. After this first brave move there is a surge of animals towards the water-hole. The zebras still hold back for a few minutes, nervously searching for predators with their acute senses of smell, sight and hearing, until they are confident that there is no danger. Stallions challenge one another and fight as they try to give their own harem access to the water.

With the arrival of the rains, a dramatic event occurs in the north-eastern section of the Makgadikgadi, called the Sua Pan. The Nata River, which rises in the highlands of Zimbabwe, flows only when there is rain. It empties its rain-fed waters into the Sua Pan, forming a second but (compared with Okavango) much smaller inland delta in the Middle Kalahari. Soon the dry lake bed is covered by a shallow sheet of water which stretches for several hundred square kilometres. The calm water merges with the powder blue of the sky, creating a land of no horizon. The waters quickly become saline as the crusty salts on the surface of the pan dissolve, and they are further concentrated by evaporation under the sun's heat. Despite this salinity, the arrival of water brings an abundance of life. As if by a miracle the warm shallows become alive with millions of tiny shrimps and other crustaceans, hatched from eggs buried in the white salt mud. Algae also flourish in the saline water.

Opposite: Common throughout the Kalahari, ostriches are able to withstand intense heat and dryness and keep cool by fluffing out their back feathers (top). They lay eggs in communal nests (bottom), but the eggs are incubated only by the major hen and her mate.

The eggs of the brine shrimp are one of the most resilient forms of life on earth. They are superbly adapted to such a harsh and unstable environment as the Kalahari salt pans. The eggs survive in the salt mud under great extremes of temperature, totally desiccated and almost inert. Biological tests on such eggs have failed to detect a metabolism (body chemistry) of one ten-thousandth of the normal levels. To all intents they are dead. They can remain in this resistant form for many years. Yet as soon as they are wet, when the salt pans flood, they hatch into delicate white shrimps that swim upside down by means of eleven pairs of feathery limbs. The quantity of brine shrimps that hatch out with the flooding of the Sua Pan defies calculation: there are millions of tonnes, constituting the base of a massive food chain.

Birds quickly learn of the temporary abundance of food in this isolated pan of the Kalahari. Greater and lesser flamingoes arrive in their thousands, sometimes even hundreds of thousands. Winged migrants, no one knows where they come from – perhaps from other large pans in Southern Africa, such as Etosha, or perhaps they travel from the soda lakes of the Great Rift Valley in East Africa, a journey of several thousand kilometres. Both species of flamingoes use their inverted beak as a pump to filter and extract their food from the salty waters. Lesser flamingoes feed on algae, while the much more numerous greater flamingoes feed on larger organisms such as the brine shrimps. Both species breed in the delta of the Sua Pan, and records show that this has been the largest recorded breeding area for greater flamingoes in Africa.

A large number and variety of wading birds and ducks forage along the muddy edges of the temporary delta near the river mouth, picking for the new aquatic life that has blossomed in the soft mud brought down by the Nata River. Species include avocets, Hottentot and red-billed teals, dabchicks, blacksmith plovers and black-winged stilts. The temporary abundance of food makes it a good time for birds to have their young, and scattered along the sandy edges of the Sua Pan are the exposed nests of many ground-nesting birds. This provides an unusually wide choice of food for the common egg-eater snake, which has no fangs and no venom, living as it does exclusively on eggs. It is a nocturnal snake and its grey, brown and white markings closely resemble those of the poisonous night adder. The suggestion of mimicry is carried further by the alarm behaviour of the egg-eater, when it twists into a series of tight S-shaped loops, which it rubs together. The scraping scales produce a hissing sound, much like the hiss of the night adder.

The head of the egg-eater is small, and the snake must dislocate its jaws in order to swallow an egg (generally smaller than a chicken's egg). Although fangless, the egg-eater has several dozen bony projections deep in its throat, with which it punctures the eggshell. The released contents of the egg pass

Baobabs occur in scattered groups around the edges of the Makgadikgadi Pans; their swollen trunks hold great quantities of water, enabling them to survive long periods of drought. Hollows in the trunks provide safe nest sites for birds such as barn owls.

Mopane woodlands (opposite) are an important habitat since their pans retain water long into the dry season. Mopane moth caterpillars (opposite bottom) feed on the leaves of the mopane tree, while a martial eagle (below) and its mate raise their young high up in a 'traditional' nest.

Elephants (opposite) roam the northern woodlands after rain, using mopane pans as watering points on their journey. An elephant which has died amongst the trees is soon detected by vultures (below). Mopane squirrels (bottom) live in family groups in tree hollows.

Relations between carnivores are never friendly, particularly at a kill.
Vultures wait impatiently while hyaenas feed (opposite). Lions (below
and opposite bottom) and spotted hyaenas are almost equal in the
feeding hierarchy – the outcome usually depends on strength of
numbers.

Zebras (below) and wildebeests (bottom right) migrate to the Makgadikgadi Pans after rain, but they only remain in the area as long as water is available. The springhare (top right), a large rodent, is a resident species which is able to survive on moisture from its food.

Elephants sometimes damage the trees they feed on; however, they also assist in the dispersal and germination of new trees. Having eaten acacia pods, the elephant passes the seeds intact (below) and they germinate in moist and nutrient-rich conditions (bottom).

Perhaps the drying pans act as a signal for nomadic buffalo (below)
to return to the permanent rivers and swamps before the interior dries
up completely.
Overleaf: Zebras at sunset.

Opposite: On reaching permanent water from the drying interior, elephants quench their thirst and lay the dust of their long journey.

81

down to the stomach, and the emptied eggshell is regurgitated in a neat package, after which the snake must realign its jaws.

At dusk flocks of white pelicans return from their feeding grounds on the Nata River and waters even further away. Fish brought in by the seasonal Nata River soon die in the saline waters of the Sua Delta, although the vast Pan provides the birds with a safe roosting place. Leaving the thermals, the pelicans wheel in the sky and eventually settle like aircraft carriers onto the glassy smooth water. As the fiery crimson sun slides over the horizon it tinges the water sky-pink, matching the dusky pink of the flamingoes that have also settled for the night in this extraordinary and timeless world.

CHAPTER FOUR
NOMADS OF THE INTERIOR

After the brief rains, the relentless heat soon leaves vast tracts of the Kalahari interior devoid of water. The small scattered pans of the grasslands, the woodlands of the sand plateau, and the saline vastness of the Makgadikgadi Pan all revert to unremitting dryness. The water-dependent animals such as zebras, wildebeests, elephants and buffaloes, which followed the rains into the interior in search of food and minerals, must return to permanent lakes and rivers. When the Kalahari was a wetter place, when fossil rivers filled with water instead of sand and small lakes carried water throughout the year, there would have been no cause for such large-scale migrations. These same species probably had a local pattern of movement to obtain water and fresh grazing. As the Kalahari became increasingly arid, so the annual treks to water became longer, culminating in journeys today of several hundred kilometres as they return to the wetter places north and south of the sand plateau.

The animal migrations of the Kalahari were not really understood by man some two decades ago. Had we known then what is becoming clear today, the sudden and tragic interruption of the migrations in the last twenty years might not have happened on such a scale. The erection of fences to control the spread of the dreaded foot-and-mouth cattle disease and comply with EEC import regulations carved up and confined large tracts of the Kalahari. People built the fences where they pleased, and inadvertently blocked the paths of tens of thousands of wild creatures to their only sources of permanent water in times of drought. The result was the tragic and wasteful loss of perhaps half of the central Kalahari's large animals. Some migratory movements still occur today, but on a much smaller scale. Many traditional routes are now blocked by fences, farms and human habitation. To the north, however, the movement of nomadic animals is still largely unhindered, although the patterns of movement are complex and still little understood.

In the immense sand plateau of the central Kalahari the only permanent waters occur in the Molopo River to the south, the Limpopo to the south-east, and a great water crescent to the north. This northern arc of water is composed of the Okavango Delta, its southern outlets Lake Ngami (now dry) and the Boteti River, and the great northern river, the Chobe, with its associated swamplands of Linyanti and the Kwando. These areas of permanent water provide a refuge for the water-dependent animals in times of severe drought, enabling a reservoir population to survive until new rains permit them to venture once more into the interior.

The movements of migratory animals are still largely a mystery. Although these nomads respond to the sight, smell and sound of distant storms and rain, no doubt much of their migratory behaviour is a traditional response passed from generation to generation. Elands and hartebeests, antelopes that wander deep into the sand dunes and grasslands of the arid south, have the instinct to migrate southwards to the Molopo River and its tributaries in times of drought. Hartebeests are grazing animals, similar in size and shape to wildebeests; however they have the trick of digging for tubers in dry periods, which makes them more hardy than wildebeests and able to inhabit the arid sandveldt. Elands are the largest of Africa's antelopes, but have the flexibility to switch to browsing the delicate leaves and shoots of shrubs as the grasses dry. They roam the sandveldt in small mixed herds until the demand for water, or the attraction of local rains, brings their numbers together to form groups of several thousand as they move southwards.

Wildebeests are the most migratory of the Kalahari's animals, occupying and vacating large tracts seemingly at random. They are well adapted to a nomadic life, especially in their breeding behaviour. Calves are able to stand and travel with the herd within minutes of being born, whereas most antelope calves have a two-week 'hiding' period in long grass, being suckled by the visiting mother. The social structure of wildebeest herds is highly variable, but in spite of their large numbers, basic social units are recognisable within the mass. Females with their young form cohesive nursery groups, while bachelor herds of young males and territorial males wander the periphery.

The wildebeest is the only large wild herbivore in the Kalahari which has to survive the dry season on a grass diet. The shape of its wide mouth and its square lips make this grazer dependent on short grass, while its occurrence in huge concentrations is not suited to feeding on a patchily-distributed food source such as the leaves of bushes. Being restricted to grass, it must constantly be on the move to find vegetation sufficiently high in nutrients and water. It is impossible for such creatures to meet their moisture requirements from grass alone during very dry periods, so they must be highly mobile in order to obtain sufficient moisture as they cross vast distances, moving from one local patch of rain to another.

As the water pans and grasses dry out, the distant sight and sound of rain beckons the wildebeests. They move towards it with unerring instinct. Heads held low, they begin their plodding march, first forming lines and then columns as more and more join the irresistible movement. Clouds of dust rise from their thudding hooves. The hanging-head posture as they follow in lines may be related to smelling their tracks, since there are glands on the hooves which may lay a scent trail which the wildebeest behind follows. Wildebeests have folded hair-lined nostrils, well adapted to blocking out the suffocating dust of thousands of animals on the move.

As they migrate, the wildebeests follow local patches of rain for water and green grass, except in extreme drought when they head for the permanent sources of water to the north. The flexibility of their movements is a result of the extremely erratic and patchy distribution of rain. Since they occur in greater numbers in the northern sandveldt, it is natural for them to move north to the water crescent formed by Lake Ngami, the Boteti River and the southern Okavango Delta. Most of this movement was blocked by the erection in 1958 of the Kuke Fence, which stretches 360 kilometres across the northern central Kalahari. The migratory instinct caused thousands of wildebeests to travel northwards as far as this barricade; their progress barred, they turned eastwards along the fence. Finally, starving and dying of thirst, they reached the fence's end and the last drops of water in the River Boteti and Lake Xau. As unnaturally huge numbers of wildebeests concentrated, the grazing, already depleted by cattle, was quickly exhausted. The result was death for thousands of animals. This occurred during the drought years from 1979 to 1983; in that last year an estimated 50,000 wildebeests died at Lake Xau. These fantastic migrations of the central Kalahari may now be a thing of the past.

Why is there an undeniable tendency for wildebeests to move north for water and south for food? They have more reliable grazing and sweeter grasses in the slightly higher rainfall areas in the north of the central Kalahari, and they are closer to permanent water. The south, however, has something the north does not – a large number of pans and salt licks. The wildebeests probably move into the arid south and the Makgadikgadi in order to obtain minerals.

There is a separate and more fixed pattern of movement by the wildebeest populations of the Makgadikgadi region. In the wet season the herds move to the short-grass plains at the palm belt edging Ntwetwe Pan, to feed on new grasses and take salts from the pans. Here most of the females have their calves. In the dry season they move to the Boteti River, an outlet of the Okavango Delta which flows towards the Makgadikgadi. Although the river can sometimes be swift and wide, during the dry season it is restricted to a series of pools. However, it is still of major importance as it is the only source of water near the Makgadikgadi and the central Kalahari sand plateau. It forms a refuge where animals can survive until the next rains. If the dry season is extended then the grasslands are rapidly depleted, and animals must trek over forty kilometres a day to get from the river to good grazing. Many die.

The zebra is another water-dependent grazer that migrates long distances in large numbers. Together with the wildebeests, zebras follow the rains to areas with lush new grass, returning once more to permanent water in the dry season. The family unit of the zebra is called a harem, because one stallion controls a number of mares and his offspring. It is well suited to a nomadic life-style. There are strong social bonds between members of a harem, which are reinforced by individuals constantly grooming each other. The pattern of zebra stripes is unique to each animal and is as important in close contact as the animal's calls are in large congregations. In these ways individuals in a group can easily recognise each other, and they are constantly on the lookout for lost members.

As family groups gather in an area of good grazing, the harem loses identity and the zebras form huge concentrations of thousands of individuals. But as soon as they are on the move again, perhaps to find water or due to the presence of a predator, the harem re-forms. Bachelor males are constantly looking for females, especially young fillies from other harems, and fierce fighting between stallions is inevitably over the ownership of a female.

Zebras once roamed the central Kalahari but they became extinct there in the early 1960s, after the first severe drought following the erection of the Kuke Fence, which prevented them reaching the waters of the north. Zebra migrations still occur north of the fence, though there are several different patterns and much is to be learned. The Makgadikgadi Pan population follows a pattern of movement similar to that of the wildebeest. After rain they travel to the short grasslands fringing the northern edges of the pans, and here the females have their foals. Zebra mothers are extremely protective of their young, and no other zebra is allowed close to the newborn. As they grow older the foals of the harem play together more, and other females will protect a foal if the mother is not around.

During the dry season the zebras are forced to leave the pans and move closer to permanent water. Like the wildebeest they move to the grasslands near the Boteti, arriving at the river to drink in the evening. The hours of darkness are spent in the acacia woodlands on the banks of the Boteti, where they are safer from lions. One animal in a family group remains standing, alert for predators, while the others sleep. The zebras leave the river before dawn to return to their feeding grounds.

Another zebra migration occurs to the north, although at one time this movement may have also included the Makgadikgadi Pan and the central Kalahari. After the rains in November, thousands of zebras congregate on the short grasslands of the Mababe Depression and the Savuti Marsh. The Mababe was once a lake, but dried with many others during the arid phase.

Until recently the Savuti channel flowed from the northern swamps of Linyanti, but this too has dried, and with it the surrounding marshes. When the Savuti received water it was the natural concentration point during the dry season for animals coming from the north, south and east. Migratory herds now concentrate on the marshes only after rain, attracted to the abundance of short grasses on the open plains nearby. Zebras and wildebeests remain on the open grasslands until the start of the dry season in May, at which time zebras leave for areas of permanent water in the northern Linyanti swamps. The wildebeests begin their wanderings a little later, in August.

The abundance of zebras and antelopes in the Savuti region supports a large and diverse population of predators including lions, leopards, spotted hyaenas and wild dogs. However there are fewer of the desert specialists found to the south, in the arid sandveldt. Zebras are formidable opponents against most predators and the harem stallion has tremendous spirit, courage and strength. He is constantly alert, protecting his family from predators. He tirelessly searches out, calls for and returns to his care any lost or lagging members of his harem. Any individual within a family group will defend its members from predators, and so far fewer zebra foals are killed compared to the young of wildebeests. Also, because of the strong co-operation among zebras in a harem, it would be disruptive if all females had foals at the same time. So they follow a different breeding strategy from wildebeest and are 'asynchronous' breeders, as opposed to wildebeests which are 'synchronous' breeders and produce their calves at the same time.

Lions and spotted hyaenas are the most common zebra predators. They hunt at night, attempting to frighten and separate an individual from its group, since a solitary zebra is a vulnerable one. Lions in this area have larger prides and smaller territories than the nomadic lions of drier regions in the Kalahari. In the Savuti region the spotted hyaena appears to be the dominant carnivore, easily stealing the kills of lions. Despite their tendency to scavenge, spotted hyaenas are highly successful predators. They hunt in large groups of perhaps twenty individuals, and against them even a bull buffalo has little chance of survival. Like their relative, the brown hyaena, these massively-built carnivores will 'cache' bones in their dens, as a food store for lean times. The ability of spotted hyaenas to crush animal bones into fine pieces plays a wider role in the ecology of certain areas. White-backed vultures feed their chicks on small bone fragments; in those areas where the spotted hyaenas have been eradicated, vulture chicks now show calcium deficiency diseases.

The highly social, pack-hunting African wild dogs are cunning predators of zebras. There are some individuals in a pack that have learnt a sure way of overpowering their formidable prey. Breeders of horses use a 'nose-twitch', a piece of leather thong which twists around and grips the upper lip of a stallion, to control him. The effect is the almost complete immobilisation of the animal. Some wild dogs use a similar trick and will leap up at a fleeing zebra, grasp the striped horse around the lip, and bring down the immobilised animal.

The patterns of zebra and wildebeest movements have changed over millennia, according to the changing climate and availability of water. Today, with so much of the central Kalahari fenced, the migrations will always be a ghost of their former selves. But in northern regions, beyond the Kuke Fence, the movements are still largely unrestricted. Although the main migratory species are zebras and wildebeests, many others undergo a seasonal dispersal. In terms of number and size, the most important of these are elephants and buffaloes. They follow a pattern of wet-season dispersal and dry-season concentration at permanent water, a pattern quite different from that of the desert antelopes, the gemsboks and springboks, which disperse in the dry season. The dry-season concentration of thousands of animals along the fringes of permanent lakes and rivers seriously depletes the vegetation, and so many animals instinctively move to the interior once the scattered pans have been recharged by the rains, travelling to fresh grasses and shrubs that have been rested and renewed in their absence.

Elephants and buffaloes once roamed the central Kalahari extensively in the wet season. In the last decade the drying of what little water was available, plus interference from people and cattle, have restricted them to the north. They occur throughout the northern region, especially along permanent waterways such as the Okavango, Chobe and their associated swamps. As soon as the rains come they leave to roam the woodlands of the north, sometimes venturing as far south as Makgadikgadi and the Boteti River. Not all populations of these animals are involved in long-distance movements or migrations. A much smaller and more local pattern of dispersal occurs within the Okavango Delta, with movements from the large sand masses and islands that penetrate its southerly reaches, into the Delta proper with the advance of the dry season.

To the north of the Makgadikgadi, stretching eastwards to the edge of the Okavango Delta and then northwards to the Chobe River, the sparse scrub and grass of the sandveldt give way to woodlands whose growth is made possible by the increasing rainfall. Slight variations in soil type, and the rise and dip of the land due to the thinly masked dunes, result in different types of woodlands. Acacia woodlands with terminalia and leadwood trees grow on the thick ridges of deep sand, while on the finer sands and clay soils mopane trees flourish; they dominate vast tracts of the country.

From the air the lines of vegetation clearly show the changes in soil type and relief. The dense woodlands of mopane trees gradually give way to stands of acacia and silver terminalia. Patches, waves and lines of wood-lands are separated by lagoons and channels of grass. The curving lines of these grasslands, looking like pools of golden water, suggest areas that were once flooded during wetter times in the past. No doubt they are old valleys and pans which still occasionally become waterlogged after rains, and so do not permit the growth of trees.

These woodlands of the north form an important habitat for many animals. The mopane woodlands are the most widespread and the most important. The mopane is also called the butterfly tree since each leaf is composed of two leaflets which look like the wings of a butterfly. They produce a cool dappled shade in the heat of the Kalahari summer. The mopanes grow best on soils with poor drainage, which is why they occur in areas of fine sand with a high clay content. They are exceptionally resistant to drought, since the tree is able to make internal adjustments to cope with a wide range of water stresses. In ideal conditions they grow tall in dense stands which form an almost continuous canopy, hence its other name of cathedral mopane. Where conditions are tougher mopanes tend to grow as shrubs.

Because of their clay soils, the mopane woodlands have pans which hold water well into the dry season, when the rainwaters of sandy regions have long since disappeared. These rain-filled pans attract zebras, wilde-beests, elephants, buffaloes and sable and roan antelopes, which wander the woodlands for many months. Wide paths, trodden by elephants over millennia, lead from one water-hole to the next. These paths lead animals to water as they venture into the dry Kalahari. Long after the rains, when the pans are almost dry, the nomadic animals gradually make the final long trek back to the rivers and swamps, using the pans as staging posts on their return journey.

The largest of the creatures that use these water-holes probably helped to create them. Elephants are constantly enlarging the pans by digging for water. They cool their skins with coatings of thick clay mud. As the mud dries, they rub it off against nearby trees, which helps remove irritating skin parasites. Some pans may have originated at the edges of the tall clay mounds of fungus termites, which are common in mopane woodlands. The termite mounds are rich in minerals (a by-product of termite saliva and clay soil). Animals come to lick at the mounds and, as they do so, they dig at its edges with their hooves in order to loosen the salts. Over a period of time a depression forms which collects water, attracting other animals that drink and wallow in the small water-hole. The clay washed down from the mounds sticks to the hides of the animals and is carried away by them, a process which continues to deepen the pans. In this way the pans are constantly being formed, maintained and enlarged by their use.

The mopane tree is deciduous, losing its leaves late in the dry season. At this time the woodlands generally are bare of leaves, the pans have dried to a cracked bed of grey clay mud, and the larger animals have returned to permanent water. The last of the year's dying leaves fall from the empty branches onto the bare sands beneath. The woodlands are at their most barren and dry. Yet even at this time there are resident creatures. Common duikers skulk through trees and bushes, surviving by eating the dry mopane leaves and browsing what little undergrowth there is. Duikers will even scavenge, perhaps feeding on the abandoned carcass from the kill of a resident pair of martial eagles. Mopane tree squirrels have nests in the gnarled hollows of the larger trees, and during the day they warm away the winter's chill by sun-basking, stretched out on a branch. The pupae (chrysalises) of mopane worms lie buried in the bare sand, waiting for the rains.

The woodlands come alive with the arrival of rain. Rivulets of water run down the grey tree trunks, form channels across the clay sands and drain into the deeper pans. With the warmth and rain the crimson leaves burst from their buds and soon the trees are covered in a lush growth as the leaves turn bright green, their butterfly shape catching the breeze and producing a cool dappled shade. A sparse growth of green grass establishes itself underneath the shady canopy.

The rains bring with them the large mammals, which leave the rivers and swamps and disperse in small groups. Moving from pan to pan, they are able to penetrate deep into the woodlands and grasslands of the north. In the early morning a mixed group of greater kudu, delicate and shy despite their great size, come down to drink. They are joined by flocks of game birds which provide the martial eagles with an abundant food source. Although these massive eagles hunt large prey such as the common duiker, and also small mammals such as mongooses and mopane squirrels, their favourite and most abundant prey are large 'game birds' such as the helmeted guineafowl and crested francolin, which come to drink at the rain-filled pans. The eagles soar at a great height, surveying a woodland territory which may cover 200 square kilometres. If hunting in a limited space, such as the small area of a water pan, the bird parachutes down steeply at great speed; on contact it shoots its long legs forward and grasps its prey, usually killing it on impact.

Buffaloes sometimes come to the pans soon after rain. Their massive black shapes emerge menacingly from the trees, curved horns held high and noses sniffing the air for signs of danger. Sable antelopes prefer to drink at midday, cautiously emerging from the shady woods and checking for predators before lowering their heads to drink. Their crescent-shaped horns, grown by both males and females, form a battalion of weapons reflected in the water of the muddy pool. In the intense noonday heat the mopane leaflets move closer together, like the folding wings of a butterfly, to reduce evaporation.

At dusk elephants follow their wide highways to the edge of the water pan, where they cool in the mud and drink their fill before another night of wandering and feeding. They like to spend time in the terminalia woodlands on the sand-dune ridges, relishing the roots of the terminalia trees as well as eating their leaves and seeds. But these areas of deep sand contain no water, so their use by elephants is restricted to times when the mopane pans are full, providing a nearby water source. In the twilight thirsty zebras hurry through the mopane woodlands towards a pan. The shapes of the branches and trunks in the thin rays of evening light act as a disruptive background to camouflage their black and white stripes. After drinking the zebras are gathered together by the barking call of their stallion, and return once more to the cover of the trees.

At night the mopane woods are a different world. They resound with the deafening noise of crickets. Bats flit over the open surface of the pans, catching insects attracted to the warmth rising from the water. Several species of bats occur in these woodlands; they avoid feeding competition by taking different sizes and species of moths and other insects. At this time of the year the mopane emperor moths emerge from their underground pupae. The mouthparts of the adult moths are not fully developed so they cannot feed – they must mate quickly before dying a few days after emerging. Females release a pheromone (chemical signal) into the air which is picked up by the large feathery antennae of the males. The males are attracted by the signal, and soon after mating the female lays her eggs on the green mopane leaves. She will die before the eggs hatch out three weeks later.

When the mopane moth eggs hatch the small green caterpillars have their first meal – their own eggshells. It is not clear why, but if they do not have this food first they are unable to feed on their normal leaf diet. There may be some substance in the eggshells which allows their digestion to cope with normally indigestible leaf material, since green mopane leaves have a high content of oils and chemicals and they smell like turpentine. Soon the caterpillars grow fat, black-spotted, green and hairless, and very large, measuring over six centimetres in length. In vast numbers, they quickly denude a tree of its leaves. The fully grown caterpillars, or 'mopane worms', provide a tasty and high-protein food for many animals, including humans. Even common duikers feed on them.

Small scale insects also lay their eggs on green mopane leaves. The eggs have a cone-shaped covering of clear sweet gum which baboons, in particular, will search for and consume.

When the mopane woodlands are still in green leaf, in the middle of the rainy season, the martial eagle pairs begin to rebuild their nests. A pair uses the same nest for many years – usually sited in the fork of the largest mopane tree in their territory. The nest is constructed of sturdy sticks and lined with leaves and small twigs. With repeated rebuilding it reaches a great size, about two metres wide and deep. The female lays a single egg in May, which hatches in June (the start of the dry season) after an incubation period of forty-eight days. The male eagle brings food to the female, who feeds their chick, but after a few weeks the female also leaves the nest occasionally to hunt. When the chick is ten weeks old it is completely feathered and able to feed itself on food brought to the nest by its parents.

Mopane tree squirrels are amongst the liveliest and most charming of the resident woodland animals. They live in groups, probably small family parties, sharing the same nest in the hollow of a mopane tree. Any strange squirrel attempting to enter the nest is immediately chased away. Their social communication is reinforced by smell and touch; they indulge in mutual marking by rubbing their scent glands against each other's bodies, and they spend a great deal of time in mutual grooming. They are agile climbers, scampering from tree to tree and sometimes hanging by their feet to reach food on the outermost branches. They also forage on the ground for ants, termites, fallen seeds and leaves.

Mopane tree squirrels fall prey to many predators – baboons, mongooses, snakes, small cats and large birds of prey. When a predator appears the entire group lines up along a branch, screaming and flicking their tails and bobbing their heads. It is an effective mobbing display which sends many embarrassed predators skulking for cover! The squirrels breed throughout the year, the male noisily chasing a receptive female before mating, although most young are born in the warm wet season when there is abundant food. The female first lines her nest hole with leaves and grass, before her confinement.

By the end of the rains many of the larger animals must venture far from the rivers and swamps in search of food. Elephants, buffaloes, zebras and wildebeests cover great distances as they explore the interior in search of fresh pastures. Some reach as far south as the Makgadikgadi, and for a brief time the big game of the north intermingles with the arid-land animals of the south. Zebras and buffaloes feed with herds of springboks and gemsboks. Less hardy animals such as the sable antelope remain in the mopane woodlands to be closer to permanent water. The herds of female sables and their young cover large wet-season ranges measuring hundreds of square kilometres. The magnificent black sable bulls are territorial and do not wander like the female herds. They remain in their territories, defending them from intruding males and waiting for female herds to pass through in order to have the chance to mate. Unlike zebras in their harems, sable antelope females are independent of the males and pass through the territories of many bulls in their seasonal wanderings. The young males leave the female herds and form bachelor groups which also wander large areas, waiting for the chance to establish their own territories when they are large enough to challenge a resident male. Only the strongest males will obtain a territory and have the chance to breed.

By June or July, in the middle of the cold dry season, the mopane woodlands have changed dramatically. At this time of year they resemble autumnal beech woods in Europe. The leaves have dried to gold and russet colours which match the papery kidney-shaped seed pods that also cover the trees. The wind scatters the dying leaves and dry seed pods, which fall to the ground in a thick carpet. Ecologically, woodlands are at their most important at this time. In the Kalahari sandveldt the pans have long since dried, the grasses are gone and the shrubs and most trees have lost their leaves. Mopanes are among the last trees to drop their leaves, and although dry they are rich in protein and phosphorus. To some animals they are more palatable in this condition than when green, and they are a vital source of winter food for many creatures. Elephants relish them and reach high to break off branches, so bringing them within the reach of smaller animals. Buffaloes, kudus, impalas and sables all feed on the drying leaves, both those still on the trees and those that have fallen to the ground. Giraffes often abandon the arid acacia grasslands and move to mopane woodlands to feed on the late crop of leaves, their patterned coats a perfect foil against the gold and grey of the trees.

The pans dry rapidly in the autumn mopane woodlands. They are the last areas of the interior to have any water at all and elephants dig holes in the clay mud to reach the moisture beneath, which collects to provide drinking water for other animals. Perhaps it is the drying pools, or perhaps the passing of another season, but somehow the nomadic animals recognise that they must soon return to the rivers and swamps before the last waters evaporate. Gradually they set off, moving from pan to pan where there are hopefully a few patches of water to sustain them on their long journey. As they leave the clay pans they carry with them the seeds of the mopane trees, stuck to their hooves by clay mud and the sticky gum-glands of the pods themselves. (The scientific name for mopane means 'seed of the light', referring to the fact that the seeds will only start to grow above ground and do not germinate buried in soil.) In this way, nomadic animals extend the range of the vital mopane woodland habitat.

The wandering herds drift away and will not be seen again until the next rains. But the woodlands are not entirely empty. Mopane worms have travelled down the tree trunk and buried themselves in the soil at the base of the tree. Here they pupate, developing through the winter into the magnificent adult moths that emerge with the next rains. Mopane tree squirrels forage on the ground, collecting and burying mopane seeds as a food store for the next dry season. The young martial eagle has been in its nest for several months and is almost ready to fly, preparing itself by stretching and vigorous wing exercises. Already it ventures onto the branch near its nest. The female brings most of its food at this stage, but she spends less time at the nest and leaves the young bird to feed itself. It may seem odd that large birds of prey such as the martial eagle raise their chicks in the cold dry season, when food is least abundant. However, there is an advantage: the young eagle will fledge by the beginning of the rains and so will be learning to feed and fend for itself when food is more plentiful.

The exact destination of the different herds of nomadic animals is still a mystery: some will return to the same dry-season refuge year after year, while others, such as buffaloes and elephants, wander more widely. Small scattered groups join together as they journey. Thousands of animals travel to the fringes of the Okavango Delta, in anticipation of the floods which replenish the dry floodplains and reach the very edges of the mopane wood-land. Many journey northwards for hundreds of kilometres to the waters of the vast Linyanti swamps and the Chobe River. In prehistoric times, the Chobe joined the Okavango and Upper Zambezi rivers to flow southwards into the Makgadikgadi pans, until subterranean movement caused it to pond back. Now it rises in Angola as the Kwando (Cuando) River and then disappears into the swampland of Linyanti, re-emerging as the Chobe River. The Chobe flows along the northern border of Botswana towards the Victoria Falls and thence into the Indian Ocean; it is a vital source of water for the nomads of the Kalahari.

Running parallel to the Chobe River is a broad belt of teak woodlands which occurs in deep Kalahari sands where mopane cannot compete, and which holds no water. This is the final barrier the animals must cross before reaching the blue waters of the Chobe. Yellow and gold leaves fall in the cold wind and, except for the pistol-cracking of dry pods, splitting as they scatter their seeds, the woods are silent and empty. There are so few animals in this waterless teak woodland that seeds depend on this scattering device rather than on animals for their dispersal.

The large herbivores pass quickly through, hastening to the river. Sable and roan antelopes, the most water-dependent animals, are the first to return to graze on the river floodplains, resting during the day in the shady forests that fringe this great river. Later zebras, wildebeests, giraffes and kudus pass through, hurrying to quench their thirst and lay the dust of their long journey in the waters of the swiftly flowing river. Buffalo herds, numbering several thousand animals, crowd on the floodplains; some have journeyed as far as the northern grasslands of the Makgadikgadi pans and back. Elephants wade

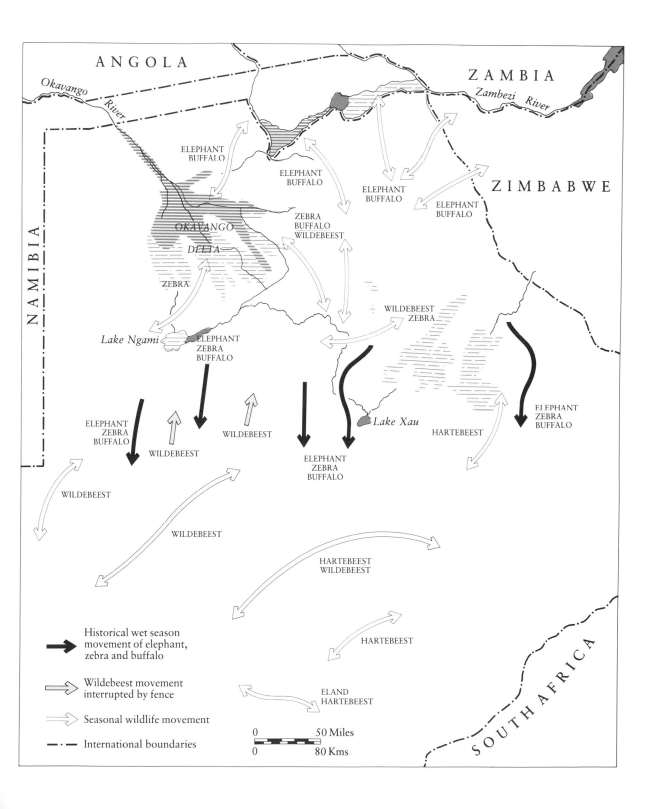

ANGOLA

Okavango River

ZAMBIA

Zambezi River

ELEPHANT
BUFFALO

ZIMBABWE

ELEPHANT
BUFFALO

ELEPHANT
BUFFALO

ELEPHANT
BUFFALO

N A M I B I A

ZEBRA
BUFFALO
WILDEBEEST

OKAVANGO

DELTA

ZEBRA

WILDEBEEST
ZEBRA

Lake Ngami   ELEPHANT
ZEBRA
BUFFALO

ELEPHANT
ZEBRA
BUFFALO

ELEPHANT
ZEBRA
BUFFALO

WILDEBEEST

WILDEBEEST

Lake Xau

HARTEBEEST

ELEPHANT
ZEBRA
BUFFALO

WILDEBEEST

WILDEBEEST

HARTEBEEST
WILDEBEEST

HARTEBEEST

Historical wet season
movement of elephant,
zebra and buffalo

Wildebeest movement
interrupted by fence

Seasonal wildlife movement

International boundaries

ELAND
HARTEBEEST

S O U T H   A F R I C A

0   50 Miles
0   80 Kms

into the water, drinking deeply while their calves play in their new-found luxury.

They join the river's permanent residents – hippopotamuses, crocodiles, impalas, Chobe bushbucks and the smaller creatures such as birds, snakes, fish and frogs. Lechwe, puku and waterbuck, three closely-related species of antelope, co-exist on the floodplains, avoiding competition by fine differences in their choice of food and their position on the floodplains. The shimmering blue waters contrast vividly with the surrounding dusty grey land. While most of the trees and bushes have lost their leaves, the winter-flowering Jessie bush provides a welcome splash of colour and a change of food for elephants and bushbuck, signalling the beginning of a season of plenty.

The dry season concentration of elephants along the Chobe River forms the highest density of elephants in the world (up to six elephants per square kilometre). This results in heavy feeding pressure on the riverine forests – particularly on the elephants' favourite tree, the knobthorn acacia. However, as long as the elephants have their freedom of movement they will disperse into the interior when the first thunder signals the rain, thus resting the riverine forests until the next dry season. Elephants are an integral part of the ecological system. By feeding on trees, they pull down branches and make food available for other creatures to browse; they disperse the seeds of trees whose germination is enhanced by starting life in moist, nutrient-rich elephant dung; and by digging water-holes they make water available to smaller animals.

By the end of the dry season there is an incredible diversity and abundance of life in the riverine forests. These forests extend along the banks of all the major rivers – the Zambezi, the Chobe, the Linyanti and the Okavango. Over thousands of years, the river systems changed their course: new swamps were formed while others dried up; channels ceased to flow and new ones were created. During these changes the forests provided food, water and shelter to a host of water-dependent creatures. They acted as a pathway along which very different forms of life could penetrate the arid Kalahari.

On its 80-kilometre journey through the Panhandle, the Okavango River meanders through papyrus swamps contained between two parallel faults.

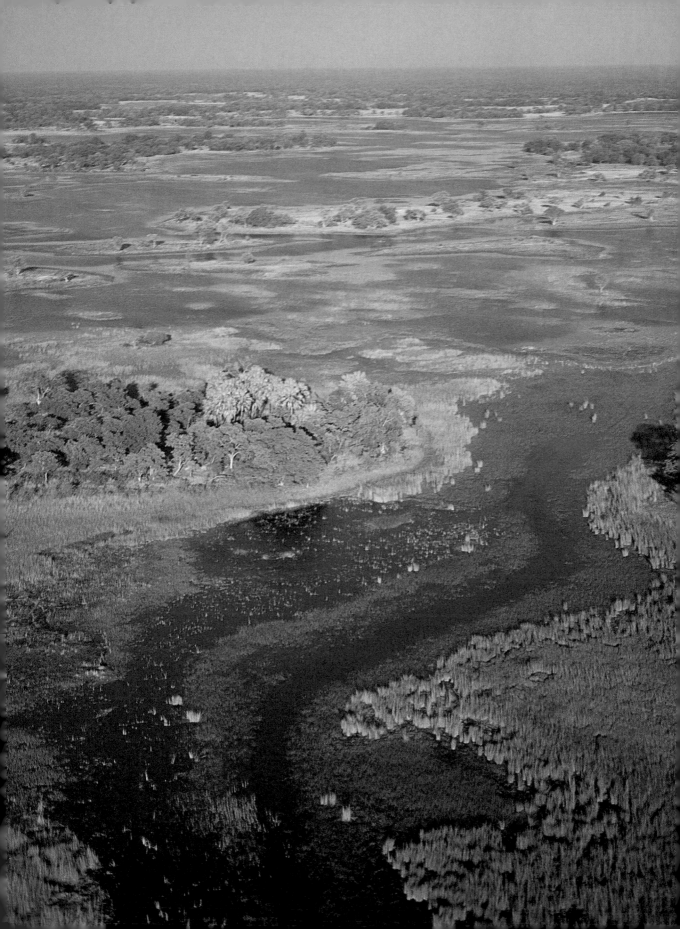

On leaving the Panhandle, the Okavango's waters spread out over the Kalahari sands (opposite), transforming the 'desert'. In spite of the luxuriant growth of papyrus (below), it is inhabited by relatively few creatures. Freshwater shrimps (bottom) survive in the peaty water by feeding on detritus trapped by papyrus roots.

Hippopotamuses and crocodiles (below) are the largest animals
occurring in the Panhandle. African skimmers nest on sandbanks on
the Okavango River (opposite), exposed during periods of low water.
Overleaf: At dusk, skimmers cut a path through the water as they hunt,
lower beak snapping shut on contact with a fish.

The sitatunga (below) is the only large mammal to inhabit the papyrus swamp. Its long hooves, which splay out as it walks, allow it to travel through the swamps with ease. Although the majestic fish eagle (opposite top and bottom), common throughout the Okavango Delta, is an adept fishing bird, it will also scavenge on the catch of other creatures.

Life abounds in the shallow, reedy backwater lagoons (opposite). Here carnivorous sundews (below left) catch insects such as dragonflies (below right); and the bell-like calls of the painted reed frog (bottom left) and the sonorous croak of the beautifully camouflaged back-striped *Rana* frog (bottom right) dominate the night.

In tranquil lagoons, water lilies (opposite top) support an intricate web of life. Pygmy geese (opposite bottom) feed on the seeds of lily bulbs, and midges (below) lay eggs in day lily flowers. Carpenter bees collect pollen from water lilies (bottom right) and take it to their nest in hollow phragmites stems.

112

The stamens of the day lily provide a meal for blister beetles (below).
The yellow night lily (bottom left), like some other flowers, 'changes' sex
to ensure cross-pollination; a visiting insect, carrying pollen from a male
flower, falls into the stigmatic fluid of the female night lily (bottom right)
and drowns.

CHAPTER FIVE
JEWEL OF THE KALAHARI

The Okavango Delta, in the midst of the Kalahari sands, is Africa's largest and most beautiful oasis. The River Okavango, which rises in the highlands of Angola, never reaches the sea; instead its mighty waters empty over the sands of the Kalahari. Here the thirstland of the south meets a blue-green wilderness of fresh water, with emerald reedbeds and towering trees. It is a natural refuge and giant water-hole for the larger animals of the Kalahari. The water gives rise to many forms of life unexpected in a 'desert' such as the Kalahari – there are fish, crocodiles basking on the sands, and hippopotamuses and swamp antelopes feeding on the vegetation. One cannot help but wonder how the Okavango Delta came to be here, in some fantastic accident of nature.

There is still much to discover about the Delta and its origins. It is the last surviving remnant of the great Lake Makgadikgadi, whose waters and associated swamps once covered much of the Middle Kalahari. It is also closely associated with the Kwando–Linyanti–Chobe swamps and river systems to the north-east. It is thought that long ago the Okavango, Chobe, Kwando and upper Zambezi waterways flowed as one massive river across the Middle Kalahari, to join the Limpopo River and then flow to the Indian Ocean. The earth movements which created the rift of the Kalahari–Zimbabwe Axis impeded this flow, causing a damming back of the giant river which resulted in the formation of a series of huge and complex swamps. As the Okavango River left the humid highlands and entered the arid flatness of the Kalahari, it slowed and dropped its sediment load. Channels became blocked and the water sought other courses, continuing to deposit its sediments wherever it travelled. Over time, some two million tonnes of sand and debris were deposited over the Kalahari sands, creating the characteristic fan shape of the Delta. The Okavango's waters still cut paths through this built-up cone and deposit their sand load, causing the channels to continue changing direction. Superimposed on these changes were the climatic fluctuations of the last million years. In arid periods these complex swamps and waterways would recede; in wetter times the myriad channels may have combined to form one vast river flowing into a huge lake – the former Lake Makgadikgadi.

Two parallel faults now control the direction in which the Okavango River enters the Kalahari Basin, in an area called the Panhandle. Other faults also direct its exit from the Delta, flowing south into the ocean of sand. As the Okavango flows over the Gomare Fault, a continuation of the Great Rift Valley of East Africa, which runs south-west to north-east, the slope of the land breaks it up into numerous channels which fan outwards over the Delta. These are blocked by two southern faults, the Kunyere and the Thamalakane, which redirect the Delta's myriad channels. The Thalamakane Fault acts as a 200-kilometre-long natural dam; here the channels abruptly change direction and join to form one river, the Boteti, which flows eastwards through a break in the fault towards the Makgadikgadi Pan. A small channel, the Nghabe River, continues south-west towards Lake Ngami, serving as both inlet and outlet depending on the strength and direction of the annual floods.

The formation of a rift between the Gomare and Thamalakane Faults probably caused the ponding back of the Okavango's waters. This earth movement, which occurred in the last million years, together with more arid climatic phases, accelerated the building of the Okavango's cone-shaped delta through further deposition. It probably also accelerated the drying of Lake Makgadikgadi. The same earth movements caused a similar ponding back of the Kwando River system, its waters escaping north-eastwards to join the Zambezi River system via the Victoria Falls.

The present Okavango is still connected to the Chobe–Zambezi River system via the Selinda Spillway. However, recent arid conditions mean that these water courses are now seldom joined. The geology of the Okavango is still inherently unstable, as the faults continue to move and earth tremors occur. Channels become filled with sand and debris, and massive plugs of papyrus interrupt their flow. The pattern of drainage in the delta will continue to change.

Rivers that do not reach the sea are called interior drainage systems. They occur typically in arid areas where water evaporates to leave an accumulation of salts as a saline pan, as in Makgadikgadi and Lake Ngami. The Okavango is unique in that it forms a freshwater delta. The reason it does so is because it has several outlets. Even though their outflow comprises only three per cent of the Okavango's inflow, this is enough to carry away most of the salts and keep the Delta's waters fresh.

In fact there are two groups of outlets: west to Lake Ngami and south and east to the Makgadikgadi Pan via the Boteti River. The reason for two main outlets is the flatness of the Delta, which gives rise to a very unstable drainage pattern. Any small change in the lie of the land will cause a shift in the direction of water flow. For example, until the 1880s the Thaoge River, to the west, carried the bulk of the Okavango's flow as far as Lake

Ngami. Now the strength of flow has shifted – whether from blockages of papyrus, or sand deposits, or a tilting of the earth's crust, is not known for sure. The result is that the eastern rivers, the Moanatshira and Mborogha, carry far more water today than they did a hundred years ago. The Boro River, which runs south-east through the centre of the Delta, remains little changed. It skirts the western edge of a massive sand island in the heart of the Delta, called Chief's Island.

Two plants dominate the Delta's perennial swamps: papyrus, a giant sedge (type of grass) which grows naturally only in Africa, and the willowy phoenix palm. They provide a fascinating record of recent changes in the limits of the perennial swamps. Papyrus, being a herbaceous species, responds more quickly to changes in water level than the phoenix, which is a woody species. The full extent of the perennial swamps along the Thaoge River, before it began to dry up this century, can be seen by the distribution of the phoenix palm, which extends much farther south than papyrus. Conversely, papyrus extends much farther east than the palm, along the Moanatshira system. This indicates the expansion of perennial swamps during this century. On the Boro River the papyrus and phoenix occur in the same places, indicating that the extent of swamp areas has remained relatively unchanged in the central Delta during this century.

The Okavango River originates in the highlands of Angola as two tributaries, the Cubango and the Cuito. It has no other catchment since the land it flows through is semi-arid Kalahari sand. After several hundred kilometres, the Okavango is guided into the Delta between two northern faults about fifteen kilometres apart. Here sand deposits have built up the river bed, causing the water to spill its bank and flood the whole area of land between the faults. The main channel meanders widely between the two parallel faults. The resulting floodplain is called the Panhandle, which on a map looks like the northern 'wrist' of the many-fingered delta 'hand'.

This perennially flooded area is covered by dense reedbeds dominated by papyrus. Here the contrast of emerald green plant life juxtaposed with the dry brown thornveldt of the Kalahari is at its most dramatic.

Although the total drainage pattern in the Delta is complex, there is an underlying simplicity in the slow and regular pulse of water which flows down each year from the Angolan highlands. South of the Panhandle the Delta fans out for many kilometres. During dry periods it is estimated to cover at least 16,000 square kilometres but in wetter years, with a heavy annual flood, the Okavango's waters can spread over 22,000 square kilometres of the Kalahari's sands. Deep water occurs in only a few channels, while vast areas of reedbeds are covered by only a few centimetres of water.

The Okavango's eighty-kilometre journey through the Panhandle is its last as a single river. It flows fast and wide, the rush and eddy of its strong current the only accompaniment to the twittering calls of birds. As elsewhere on the Delta, there is a silent but continual battle between the jungle growth of papyrus and the uncolonised areas of open water. In the Panhandle the river's flow is strong enough to hold back the advance of the vegetation at its edges, and the papyrus bends submissively over its waters, feathery heads dragged with the current. Sometimes the river swings past a spit of the mainland, whose edges are lined by dense forests of fig, ebony and giant acacia. These are the daytime perches of fish eagles and the night roosts of fishing owls; genets and civets may also prowl here. The Panhandle is the domain of swamp specialists. Hippos, crocodiles and predatory fish live in the main channels, while the papyrus swamps have their own specialised forms of animal life. Only in the main delta does the abundance of islands and flooded grasslands permit an abundance of Africa's larger animals.

The luxuriant growth of papyrus is surprising, occurring as it does on impoverished Kalahari sands and in fresh waters that contain equally few nutrients. The success of this species, one of the fastest-growing plants on earth, lies in its ability to absorb nutrients even when they occur in very low concentrations. An additional form of the nitrogen essential for growth comes from microscopic bacteria and algae found between the scale-leaves of papyrus, and in moist soils. These microbes take nitrogen from the air and make it available to the plant. They are unable to survive in swamps permanently submerged by water so the flood regime of the delta, which allows for a period of dryness, is of great importance to the nutrient system of the swamps. The papyrus also uses the specialised 'Carbon-4' pathway of photosynthesis, capturing the sun's light energy more effectively than many other plants.

At the start of summer the spiky flower heads of papyrus, called 'umbels', produce thousands of seeds which fall into the river as they ripen, to be swept downstream. A few will become embedded in mud and germinate; this is one way that papyrus spreads. But in a reedbed it grows and reproduces from its matted root and rhizome system. The thick rhizomes (submerged stems) that constitute the papyrus beds send up new shoots at regular intervals. The shoots have an astonishingly quick life-cycle: within ninety days they have grown, matured and died. But the process is continual, and as one shoot dies so the papyrus withdraws its nutrients and uses them for others. This economy of nutrient cycling is another key to the plant's abundant growth.

Insects capitalise on the continual ageing and regrowth of the stems. Sap-sucking bugs such as aphids colonise the shoots when they are young and green. As the papyrus matures the multiple spikes make suitable homes for predatory insects such as beetles and preying mantises, which feed on the aphids. As the plant reaches old age spiders spin webs in the spiky umbels, hoping to trap mayflies and dancing midges that have hatched from the water. As the umbel withers its insect residents do not die, for there are thousands of other shoots going through the same life-cycle.

Papyrus is a difficult habitat for larger creatures; moving through it is almost impossible. The dense stems tower overhead and are as tightly packed as the tree canopy of an impenetrable jungle. The stems are fibrous, low in nutrients and difficult to digest. The roots and rhizomes form floating mats beneath which sediments and organic matter are trapped, but they are so loose and spongy that any creature larger than a rat sinks through. In the water below papyrus, conditions are just as difficult for aquatic life. Little light penetrates through the jungle of stems and roots, and the continual dying of its vegetation creates a build-up of organic debris, with the result that the waters are acidic and low in oxygen.

The creatures that need fewest specialisations to use the papyrus swamps are birds, since they are able to fly elsewhere to feed. They use the reeds to hide in, to build nests in, and occasionally as food, but the papyrus swamp is a preferred habitat for only a very few species. Weavers and red bishops tear off the rays from the umbels to weave their domed nests. Red bishop males mate with up to seven females each. When a male has built the main structures of several nests he calls and displays to females in his brilliant red breeding plumage. The females then line the nests with soft grass flowers, and incubate and feed the young while the male defends the territory. The plucked papyrus heads make good vantage points from which to display to females or watch for predators. These birds probably nest high in the reeds to improve ventilation and remove the excess water vapour associated with swamp life.

Some birds simply use the papyrus reeds as a handy perch or a resting place while on a journey. On rare occasions the coppery-tailed coucal can be seen sunning itself on the top of a mass of papyrus umbels. It is a secretive bird, although its deep bubbling call is an evocative early-morning sound in the reed-lined channels of the Delta.

Nesting in reedbeds has obvious advantages against larger predators, but snakes such as the boomslang move easily through reeds to rob nests of chicks and eggs. The coucal is also a notorious killer of nestlings it finds during skulking trips through the reedbeds. Swamp birds like the little bittern are superbly camouflaged as they stand frozen, beaks reaching skywards, the stripes on their necks resembling the long fluted stems of papyrus and reeds. Numerous birds frequent the river edges of the papyrus swamps, fishing in the main channel. They include pied kingfishers and various herons such as goliath, squacco and green-backed herons.

Several rodent species are able to live in the reedbeds, although none stays permanently in the marshy ground of the floating papyrus mats. Their burrows tend to be in thickets of the aquatic grasses and reeds associated with papyrus, which are rooted on the banks of rivers and channels. Being herbivorous the rodents feed on the shoots of young papyrus and reeds. The largest is the greater cane rat, which as a rodent is surpassed in size only by the dry-land porcupine. Greater cane rats live in family groups, and when alarmed the male warns his family by whistling loudly and thumping his back feet – no doubt this also alarms a potential predator. They are good swimmers if forced into water but they usually forage on land, forming distinct tunnels or 'runs' through fallen reeds and grasses. The runs hide their movements and make travelling though dense reedbeds much easier. They are also used by smaller aquatic rodents which would find it difficult to create their own tunnels. Both the large vlei rat and the shaggy swamp rat share the runs of cane rats, and also feed on the new shoots of reeds and grasses.

The elusive and shy swamp antelope, the sitatunga, is the only large mammal able to inhabit the papyrus reedbeds and also feed on them. The sitatunga occurs in swampy habitats in Central and Eastern Africa, and the Okavango Delta is its most southerly distribution. It is found widely in the northern part of the delta but probably reaches its highest concentration in the Panhandle, due to the abundance of swamp habitat. Related to bushbucks and kudus, the male sitatunga has the impressive curved horns that characterise its family of antelopes. It is a large species, the male weighing over a hundred kilograms. Despite its size it is able to inhabit the papyrus reedbeds because its long hooves, nearly twice the length of the hooves of a similar-sized antelope, splay out as it walks. This makes it possible for the sitatunga to traverse matted reedbeds and soft marshy gound with ease. Also, like other antelopes living in places of thick cover, sitatungas have raised hindquarters which give them a slow, loping gait and allow them to force their way carefully through the dense reeds with the minimum of noise.

Little is known about the social behaviour of sitatungas, which is perhaps a reflection of the habitat they live in. They are essentially solitary creatures, and although they form temporary feeding groups of up to six individuals, there is little interaction between them. The strongest social tie is between the female and her young, who will remain together until the calf is three-quarters grown. Sitatunga calves are born on a platform of flattened reeds and remain hidden in their refuge for many weeks, the female visiting to suckle her calf twice a day. Like many antelopes, the young have a 'hiding' instinct and remain motionless in their refuge if a predator comes close.

Sitatungas feed mainly in the early morning and evening following well-worn interconnecting pathways through the papyrus and reeds to their feeding areas. They tend to avoid hippo channels, probably because these are also used by large crocodiles. They sometimes move to small islands to feed at night, and they are attracted to burnt areas where the new reed shoots are more palatable and nutritious. Sitatungas are the only large mammal to exist on a diet of papyrus, although they also feed on grass and other reeds. Their diet and movements in the Panhandle are dictated by the fluctuating water level caused by the flood regime. During periods of high water they move nearer the mainland, where there is a wider variety of foods available. When the water level is low, cattle move onto the floodplains and so the sitatungas move deep into the central swamps, existing mainly on the young shoots of papyrus and their feathery culms. This antelope will reach up and hook a tall stem beneath its outstretched chin; once the stem is bent over within reach, the animal bites it halfway through, making it easier to browse on the more tasty umbels. Because of the rate at which papyrus grows, it is not long before a heavily browsed area is once more productive. Also, there is little feeding competition!

The heat of the day is spent lying up on a platform of flattened papyrus stems, which the sitatungas make by trampling them down, or on a grass island in the cool shallow waters of a quiet lagoon. They move their resting places every few days, perhaps so that predators cannot predict their movements too accurately. When alarmed the male sitatunga bounds through the reedbeds with chin held high and his horns resting along his back, presumably to prevent them becoming entangled in the dense stems and umbels. If they are threatened they tend to sink low into the floating mats and freeze, hoping to avoid detection – indeed, their shaggy brown coats render them remarkably well camouflaged in the swamps. When near open water they sometimes dive in, remaining there for long periods with their nostrils above the surface, until the danger passes.

Although young sitatungas are taken by pythons, and adults are sometimes preyed on by lions and leopards on the islands, their main predators are crocodiles. In the Panhandle these reptiles reach enormous sizes, with some monsters five metres in length and of considerable age. Lazy and prehistoric-looking, they bask on the sandbanks of the wide Okavango River as it meanders southwards to an uncertain destination.

The sandbanks are exposed only for a brief period in the low flood, from September to January. Female crocodiles lay their eggs in the sand, when water levels reach their lowest, in late September and early October. Hatching occurs in January, before the water rises with the floods and covers them. Otherwise the eggs will drown. The crocodile 'nests' are secluded from the main river by a wall of papyrus and reeds. They are usually located on sandbanks along hippopotamus paths, since the trampling activities of hippos help create suitably open sites. The female crocodile digs a hole and lays the eggs, which are then covered again. The incubation period is ninety days (roughly the life-cycle of papyrus). During this time the female remains nearby, to protect the eggs from notorious nest-robbers such as the Nile monitor lizard. When the eggs hatch she uncovers the nest and gently takes the young in her mouth, carrying them to a calm backwater. Since hatching coincides with the rise in water level, new small pools become available to the young crocodiles, away from the dangerous main channel. The maternal care of the crocodile seems surprising in such a prehistoric-looking creature that has been on earth for 200 million years, more or less unchanged.

The young crocodiles feed mainly on insects, in particular dragonflies, which they neatly snap from reeds and sedges. Beetles, giant water bugs and freshwater crabs are also important in their diet. Few of the young survive, however, for they have numerous predators – vultures, monitor lizards and even the sharp-toothed catfish. As they increase in size they begin to hunt fish, their main prey towards the middle of their life. Squeakers are the most numerous fish taken, perhaps because of their abundance, although small crocodiles are often killed by the lethal three-pronged barbs of the squeaker. Larger catfish and bream are also eaten.

When the crocodiles are two metres or more in length they begin to hunt larger mammals, in particular sitatungas, goats and cattle. During low water many cattle graze along the exposed floodplains and this rich diet might account for the extraordinary size and girth of some of the Panhandle's crocodiles! Surprisingly, even at this size they also feed heavily on plant matter such as the seeds of the phoenix palm and papyrus roots. Sandbanks do not occur in the Delta proper, and the Panhandle is the major breeding ground for the Okavango's crocodile population. So far, over one hundred breeding sites have been identified. Many young crocodiles leave the Panhandle and migrate into the Delta, to new feeding areas.

The exposed sandbanks are also important breeding sites for African skimmers, which fly south to the Panhandle to breed during the low water from September to December. After an elaborate and graceful courtship display, the pair mate and begin to excavate a shallow depression in a sandbank. Here they lay their eggs, the male and female taking turns to incubate them in the blazing sun, occasionally cooling them with breast feathers that have been immersed in the river. The well-camouflaged chicks are sometimes left unguarded as the parents go fishing, although the adults will dive-bomb potential predators even as large as fish eagles. The common sandpiper forages on the sandbanks, scavenging scraps of fish from nests of young skimmer chicks.

The skimmers make a lovely sight as they fly gracefully over the wide calm waters of the Okavango River. Their long wing-span makes them look deceptively large, for they are extremely light birds with long flight feathers that hold them aloft as they skim a few centimetres above the water's surface. They have a number of special adaptations for feeding. The lower part of the beak is longer than the upper part and is hollow, with sharp upper and lower edges that cut a path through the water. When a fish is located the lower part of the beak is raised against the upper, clamping the fish firmly. Because they fish at dusk and dawn, and at night, their eyes are adapted to low light conditions. Like a cat they have vertical pupils which widen to admit more light as it becomes darker.

In the papyrus swamps, fish and other aquatic life have to contend with low light, high acidity and low oxygen levels. These conditions are intolerable to one of the Delta's largest predatory fish, the tiger fish. The swiftly-flowing main channels and large lagoons in the upper Delta are the domain of this large characoid, a relative of the piranha, for it needs a constant supply of freshly oxygenated water. As the floods subside in the lower Delta the smaller types of fish and the juveniles of larger species must leave the floodplains and reedbeds and return to the main system. Here they concentrate in mixed shoals, grouping presumably to decrease the risks of predation. As they move upriver they are heavily preyed on by tiger fish.

The dark peaty root mats of papyrus beds demand a completely different set of adaptations. Creatures here must be able to tolerate darkness and low oxygen conditions. The giant water bug compensates for the lack of oxygen by pushing the small breathing tube at the rear of its body above the water surface. It sucks up air, which is then trapped beneath its wing covers, to be used as it hunts dragonfly larvae and tadpoles underwater. The larvae of the lake fly live in the muddy bottom of the inner swamps during the daytime, migrating to the surface at night to feed on plankton. The larvae are an important food for many fish, which follow them to the surface at night to feed, or take the pupae when they are about to hatch into adult flies. Because of the larval feeding habits their blood contains much oxygen, which in turn supplies the fish with extra oxygen in this oxygen-poor environment.

The papyrus root mats are dark and safe places where smaller fish hide from predatory tiger fish, crocodiles and voracious sharp-toothed catfish which inhabit the swiftly-flowing main river. The spiny eel is small enough to live among the fine root hairs that extend beneath papyrus rhizomes, usually where the rhizome extends into a channel and the water is better oxygenated. These are not true eels; they are named for their eel-like shape and the tiny row of spines along the back. Hiding during the day, they emerge at dusk to feed on small freshwater shrimps, fly larvae and other small insects. The shrimps are abundant in papyrus roots, where they feed on rotting debris trapped within the root mat.

Many smaller species of fish, such as the thin-faced bream, as well as the juveniles of larger species, hide in the papyrus edging the main channels. A strange-looking mormyrid known as the bulldog fish takes refuge in the roots by day, only coming out to feed at night in the more open backwaters.

These fish communicate by weak electrical signals and they feed on insects and worms, with the 'trunk' – the strange fleshy bulbous lower jaw – probably helping to feel for prey in the mud.

Each year, just before the floods, thousands of catfish migrate up the main channel of the Okavango in the upper Delta. Even the bulldog fish are not safe, hiding in the dense papyrus mats. The 'Catfish Run' is a strange phenomenon, unique to the Delta, which has probably evolved in response to the annual floods. It occurs during low water and may be an intensive feeding period for the catfish just before they move out onto the floodplains of the Panhandle, where they spawn during the floods in January and February. Each day as many as four distinct catfish runs may take place simultaneously in different parts of the river. The fish travel two to four kilometres per day, gradually moving upstream. The main species is the sharp-toothed catfish, a large predator averaging a metre in length. Normally it lives out in the main channel, but it congregates in big shoals at this time of year. It is joined by the blunt-toothed catfish, which has left the drying floodplains as the lower Delta's waters slowly receded, moving into the main channel and changing its diet from shellfish to fish.

During the 'Catfish Run' the large catfish shoal together and travel northwards along the main channels, moving through the Panhandle where they will spawn some months later. They hunt on the surface along the banks of the papyrus, where they thrash their bodies against the plants and frighten the hiding fish out into the main river. The frenzied activity of this 'pack-hunting' can be seen from far away as the water seems to boil. The activity attracts huge flocks of fish-eating birds such as fish eagles, cormorants, darters, herons, kingfishers and egrets. They follow in the wake of the hunting shoals of catfish, picking up the small fish as they dart into the channels. Crocodiles and snakes are also attracted to the area, while tiger fish lurk around the periphery, snapping up fish as they try to escape. Tiger fish prey heavily on bulldog fish and it is a mystery how they detect them in the melee. It may be by the electrical signals that the bulldogs discharge in fright.

During the day the swamps are quiet apart from the occasional calls of coot-like gallinules or the twittering of pied kingfishers. As dusk falls the cricket chorus begins, punctuated by the tinkling of reed frogs and the croaking of toads. As the sun sinks, skimmers elegantly cut a path with their beak through the mercury-smooth waters of the wide and winding Okavango. A strange popping sound, sometimes heard deep in the papyrus swamps, is the sound of sitatungas biting the spongy stems of papyrus so that they can browse on the feathery umbels.

On the second or third night after a full moon a strange event occurs. The surface of the river and the warm swamp air is alive with millions of swarming lunar mayflies. Whiskered terns swoop over the water to feed on this temporary abundance. The lunar mayflies live their larval life in silk-lined burrows in the fibrous stems of papyrus. Each month, around the time of the full moon, they emerge as winged adults for only a few hours, to mate before they die. The reason for this synchronised mass emergence is still a mystery, though it could be related to 'safety in numbers' in an area with large numbers of predators.

A creature of the night, and perhaps a symbol of all that is special about the Okavango Delta, is the magnificent Pel's fishing owl. These rufous-coloured owls are entirely nocturnal and superbly-adapted fishing birds. Solitary or living in breeding pairs, their preferred roosts are in the tall mokutshumo and fig trees that grace the banks. In ideal conditions, with large roosting and fishing trees overhanging open water, a pair of Pel's fishing owls may have a home range as small as one square kilometre. However the abundance of swamps as opposed to islands no doubt restricts the number of suitable territories. The owls are difficult to see in their roosts, but should one become conspicuous during the day it may be threatened by the resident fish eagle, which may even strike the owl. Usually, however, the nocturnal habits of the owl and the diurnal habits of the eagle enable both of these large fishing birds to live in the same area without undue competition.

As darkness falls the owls leave their roost. A pair may hunt together, fishing from a sandbank, but the best perch is the low branch of a large tree which overhangs the river, about one or two metres above the surface. From this vantage point, overlooking an area of still water, the owl waits for a passing fish. On seeing a potential prey it swoops, or more literally drops, into the water feet-first, with eyes shut at the moment of impact. The long curved claws and tiny spines on the undersides of the feet are adaptations for holding slippery fish. The Pel's owl is a skilful fishing bird, catching prey of up to two kilograms, and eating almost nothing but fish. The feeding perch of this owl can be detected by the discarded skulls of squeakers and other catfish on the ground below. It is a secretive bird and its booming call in the deep of the night, during the few hours before dawn, is the only signal of its presence.

CHAPTER SIX
PLACE OF REEDS

Dawn arrives quietly in the reed-lined channels. Towering walls of papyrus and rushes block out the sun's early morning rays. The river water, still in shadow, glistens almost like oil as it slides and eddies along its relentless course, the mists of early morning still rising from its surface. The only evidence of the channel's strong flow is the curve and rustle of floating hippo grass as the water sweeps by. The land is so flat that the first rays of sunshine fall only on the *Hyphaene* palms, standing tall above the reeds on the occasional termite-mound 'island', their dark fronds etched against a cobalt sky like frozen fountains. By seven o'clock the sun has climbed high enough to reach the western banks of the channels, filling the reedbeds with filtered light. Suddenly the place is alive with the songs of birds.

The moment the Okavango River leaves the restraining arms of the Panhandle it spills and spreads over the sands of the Kalahari in a wide fan-shaped delta, dominated by swampland in its upper reaches. A few main channels, lined by tall reeds, carry the bulk of the Okavango's water through the delta like great aqueducts; some travel south, while others flow east until a fault line in the landscape redirects them southwards again. The occasional lagoon reaches a depth of a few metres, but only the main channels bear any resemblance to the former size of the Okavango River. Some twenty to thirty metres wide, and up to five metres deep, the channel beds are composed of Kalahari sand and are largely devoid of vegetation due to the swiftness of the current. Were it not for the size and speed of these channels, the Okavango's waters would be lost even sooner to the heat of the sun.

Apart from the channels the northern delta is covered by shallow water, flooded grasslands, backwater swamps, ox-bow lakes and hidden lagoons, mostly interconnected by narrow waterways. The region is a complex of perennial and seasonal swamps and floodplain grasslands. The seasonal swamps are only flooded during high water, when the rivers spill their banks and inundate vast tracts of land. The floodplains are only intermittently covered, depending on rainfall or the direction and intensity of the river's flow that year. Change is the essence of the Okavango's waterways.

Papyrus, having dominated throughout the Panhandle, is ousted by other reeds and sedges as the swamps become less permanent. Miscanthus grass occurs in shallow flooded sites and occupies vast areas called flats in the middle of the delta. This grass grows in thick tussocks, some three or four metres high, and is virtually impenetrable. Similarly its cylindrical spiky leaves are inedible to all creatures, unless recently burnt. Miscanthus is one of the first plants to colonise deposits of sediment or peat accumulation, and as such it plays a major role in the gradual change from swamp to floodplain. However only a few creatures, such as nesting birds, can make use of its long pointed leaves.

Bullrushes are the least abundant of the tall reeds, but grow in patches here and there in shallow lagoons and backwater swamps. Their tall strap-like leaves provide a more open habitat than papyrus, permitting the delicate snow-lily to spread over the water's surface and grow in the dappled light. Phragmites reeds dominate the sluggish waters of medium depth, where they fringe river channels away from papyrus areas. Unlike floating papyrus swamps, phragmites and bullrush reedbeds are rooted and generally provide a more open and airy habitat. The phragmites reeds are the tallest of the swamp plants, towering five metres above the water. Only elephants will eat their tough fibrous root system; the tall bamboo-like stems are inedible even to those giants, but they do provide the perfect home for an industrious insect, the carpenter bee.

The carpenter is adapted to a wide range of conditions throughout Africa, but it has learned to make good use of the Okavango's abundance of hollow dry phragmites stems. The female bee bores a hole in the stem and prepares a nest, polishing and smoothing the inside. The shavings from her labours provide a 'plug' with which she partitions each egg in a cell as it is laid along the stem. Within each cell she leaves a ball of pollen and nectar – food for the developing larva. Water lilies provide the most abundant food source, although in winter, when the water lilies die back, the bees must travel to islands to visit winter flowers such as mistletoe or the early blossoms of trees like the sausage tree.

There are many predators of the carpenter bee, and against the yellow bee-pirate wasp they have little defence. The wasp waits, often well camou-flaged in a yellow night lily, ready to pounce on a visiting bee, which it stings to death. In true pirate spirit the wasp squeezes the dead bee to extract every drop of fluid and nectar, before flying off with the carcass, in which it will lay its eggs. Carpenter bees also fall victim to that common ubiquitous predator, the tiny but voracious brown ant. Although the bee's watery home is largely safe from ant attack, a fallen branch or reed may form a 'bridge' along which ants can invade. But in this case the carpenter bee has a good defence: the adult bee inside the reed blocks the circular entrance by pressing its abdomen against the hole, which is seemingly tailor-made for just that purpose.

Apart from the main channels, the water appears almost directionless as it meanders and spreads over the flat Kalahari sands, slowly seeping through the reedbeds. Channels branch into waterways; some lead to hidden lagoons, others lead nowhere as they are lost in a maze of thick towering reeds. Few creatures can push their way through these channels. Humans still travel best in the traditional wooden dug-out canoe, the 'mokoro', used for millennia by the swamp dwellers. Even with a mokoro progress is suddenly stopped by a thick plug of vegetation, although a pair of pygmy geese may fly frustratingly overhead and land on a lily-covered lagoon only metres beyond the impenetrable wall of reeds. Lagoons like this probably have their own waterways weaving around them, a seemingly independent system of channels, but in truth all the waters are connected as they pass freely through the reedbeds.

The airborne creatures are the true masters of the Okavango. They can fly over the banks of reeds, use the fibrous stems and unpalatable leaves for nests and homes, and travel effortlessly from lagoon to backwater to island in search of food. They are by far the most abundant and diverse creatures in the Okavango: birds, dragonflies, mayflies, midges and bees, they fill the air with their comings and goings and vibrant colours. The nocturnal dragonfly swoops low along the waterways at dusk; in the fading light, its huge iridescent green eyes spot the midges on which it feeds. At night small bats swoop along the narrow channels, scooping moths and insects from the surface of the water.

In the Panhandle the waters of the Okavango tend towards murkiness, carrying massive loads of sediments and coloured by the peaty debris of the papyrus swamps. But the vast expanses of reedbeds act as a filter, catching the suspended solids and slowing the water so that they are deposited. The result is the clear water of the Delta at the lower limits of the perennial swamps, best appreciated in the Okavango's lagoons. Here the water, diverted from the swift main channel, forms tranquil pools where the current is slow enough to allow the establishment of underwater plants. Sometimes the lagoons, or 'madiba', are ox-bow lakes, cut off from the main channel by the ever-changing reedbeds. Since the main food source in this aquatic habitat is vegetation and detritus (rotting debris), the majority of the eighty fish species in the Delta are herbivorous. Most of these feed on small particles, detritus and algae. The red-breasted bream, which abounds in the lagoons, is the only delta fish which specialises on flowering water plants, and new lily leaves are a particularly favoured food.

Predatory fish are less abundant in the lagoons, although the tiger fish lives here, where it is territorial even during the non-breeding season. The tiger fish is a powerful hunter, with a mouth dominated by a vicious set of large conical teeth. The striped robber fish is one of its main victims, as well as cichlid fish too large to escape to the safety of the backwater swamps. Some tiger fish also take catfish, and it seems they are generally opportunistic feeders – they have even been found with poisonous snakes in their stomachs.

One of the few fish able to live alongside the tiger is a species of relatively small catfish, the 'squeaker'. The name comes from the grating sound it makes when disturbed or captured. Squeakers are well protected by strong spines on each of their dorsal and pectoral fins, which are sharply barbed and can be locked by the fish into a completely rigid position. Small crocodiles and tiger fish have been found dead with the three-pronged barbs from a squeaker locked firmly in their gullets.

The reed cormorant, however, has discovered how to deal with these lethal barbs. The squeaker is nocturnal, coming out after dark and using its finely divided sensory barbels ('whiskers') to detect insect larvae and worms. It feeds upside down, either under logs or at the water's surface; by day it remains hidden beneath logs, where many squeakers will hide together. Being sluggish they are easy prey for the reed cormorant and form its major food source. The squeaker's head is protected by a thick bony shield which even the voracious tiger fish cannot break, but the reed cormorant has a unique method of immobilising the fish. The bird dives underwater, searching beneath logs to locate a squeaker, and then brings the squeaking catfish to the surface. Here it manipulates the fish in its beak until it can thrust the lower beak into the squeaker's head from behind, through the gills. This technique kills the squeaker, before it is able to erect and lock its fatal barbs.

The clear waters and open expanses of lagoons are among the most beautiful and peaceful places in the Okavango. This habitat is the realm of the fish eagle, which usually pairs for life. Each pair defends a territory which includes a sizeable stretch of water and suitable trees for nesting and perching. They attack trespassing eagles near the ground, although in the 'upper air' all individuals may soar and glide freely. As they perch majestically on the branch of a favourite tree, their haunting cries are one of the most evocative sounds of the Delta. Fish eagles hunt tiger fish, large bream and pike, although when the opportunity arises they are not above scavenging the kills of other creatures.

The low nutrient content of the Okavango's waters gives rise to an unusual but abundant submerged plant, the bladderwort of which there are a dozen species in the Delta. Described as a 'very aberrant organism', it is rootless and has little distinction between leaf and stem. The thousands of air-filled bladders are the secret of its success since they trap food – mosquito larvae. The bladderwort is carnivorous. The mouth of each bladder has several tiny bristles which, when touched by a passing animal, cause the trap to expel water. This creates a suction effect which draws in the animal, if it is small enough. Digestion in the bladder trap is the work of microbes living

Opposite: Water (gomoti) fig islands provide suitable nest sites for a great
variety of birds. Large birds, such as yellow-billed storks (top) and
maribou storks, nest on the tree canopy, while the smaller purple heron
(bottom left) nests in the lower branches. The vulnerable maribou chicks
(bottom right) rely on their parents to protect them.

there, as well as enzymes secreted by the plant. The carnivorous habit ensures
that the plant obtains the nutrients, particularly nitrogen, which it would
otherwise lack.

Another common inhabitant of the lagoons is the white-flowering
water chestnut. This aquatic plant thrives where the main stream slows to
enter a lagoon and deposits its sediment load. Its feathery roots give way to
a rosette of heart-shaped surface leaves, held up by air bladders which act
as flotation chambers. The most unusual feature of the water chestnut is
the seed pod with its massive two-pronged barbs. These stick to animal fur
or skin as an aid to seed dispersal, but their size seems to indicate evolution
towards one dispersal agent in particular, the hippopotamus. Only
the hide of the great 'water horse' would require a barb of that size to
penetrate it!

Hippos are territorial creatures. Living in mixed herds, they occupy the
lagoons during the day and move out to the islands at night to graze on
grasses. As they travel along well-worn paths, prominent trees are frequently
dung-marked by the dominant male to proclaim his territory. Their daily
movements from the lagoons through swampland to the islands create
pathways through otherwise impenetrable reeds. These 'hippo paths' are
used by many creatures including man, helping to make the swamps navigable.

The other mammals that commonly occur in lagoons are otters. There
are two species in the Okavango Delta, the ubiquitous Cape clawless otter
and the spotted-necked otter. The former is the larger and is well adapted
to travelling over land, so it usually occupies areas closer to shore. The
spotted-necked is more common in the remote lagoons. The otter's body
design, streamlined and slender, is so well adapted to water that it moves
clumsily and slowly on land; most of the time it spends fishing the lagoons.
Family parties of two parents and their two or three young are often seen
porpoising through the water around the lagoon fringes as they hunt for
fish, frogs and crabs. A catch is usually consumed on the spot, prey clasped
between forepaws as the otter floats on its back. The home range of an otter
family covers one or two lagoons, as well as the backwater swamps where
they retire to groom, rest and play. A swimming otter may suddenly disappear through a wall of papyrus, but beyond this seemingly solid barrier
is a secret and important part of the Delta – the backwater swamp.

Throughout the upper Delta the open lagoons and channels are backed
by shallow swampy areas that are constantly recharged with fresh clear
water from the main system, since there is a free flow above the papyrus
rhizomes. Within a backwater there may be small tussocks of grass on
hummocks of land, forming small islets on which otters can secretly bask and
play. Densely covered by reeds, sedges, lilies and other aquatic vegetation, the

backwaters contain a myriad of small-animal life. Here the competition is no less vibrant or dramatic than among the antelope herds on the grasslands: the eternal struggle to eat and avoid being eaten while successfully breeding for the future.

In the summer months, from September to April, the backwater swamps are full of frogs, dragonflies, fish and aquatic insects. Mosquito larvae flourish in the warm waters, and they in turn feed an intricate web of carnivores. Dragonfly and damselfly larvae, restricted to a life under water for a year, until they undergo metamorphosis into adults, are voracious feeders on the larvae. So, too, are small fish. Reed frogs are also abundant in the backwater swamps, and the long reed frog, a miniscule pale-green amphibian, feeds almost exclusively on mosquitoes.

Reed frogs do not hibernate during the cold winter, though they become inactive during this period, and more resistant to desiccation. The males begin calling in the early warmth of spring, and with the first rains the females appear, attracted to a vocal male. On summer nights, the bell-like calls of the painted reed frog and the high-pitched squeaky rasp of the long reed frog can reach a deafening crescendo as they vie for the attention of females. Long reed frog males are particularly pugnacious and a territorial male will fight viciously in an attempt to maintain his place on a slender reed, which he clasps with the suction pads on his feet. Neighbouring males attempt to clamber up the reed, which the caller defends with a series of karate kicks, kidney punches, left hooks and body squeezes. The battle is ferocious for a creature less than two centimetres long, though the kicking legs and flailing arms stretch to twice that length. After a struggle the victorious male claims the top of the reed and, puffing out a translucent green throat, signals his dominance – until the next frenzied skirmish.

By day the reed frogs can barely be seen as they cling to a swaying reed or the underside of a leaf overhanging the water. The pale green of the long reed frog provides excellent camouflage, while the painted reed frog has a more colourful pattern of brown, pink and white, with great individual variation. The skin of these frogs is sensitive to light intensity, and in the noonday heat they curl into a tight ball while their skin fades to white, presumably to help reflect heat. Reed frogs are eaten by a large number of swamp dwellers, from herons, giant kingfishers and crakes, to snakes, fish and dragonfly nymphs.

The densely vegetated backwater swamps provide small fish with a safer habitat than the open lagoons. Abundant food and high summer temperatures allow the rapid growth of young fish, but they must tolerate the resulting low oxygen levels of warm water. Top-minnows cope by living near the surface of the water, where oxygen levels are highest. Between two and four centimetres long, and with large iridescent blue eyes, they feed on small insects that fall into the water. But this life-style, so close to the surface, makes them vulnerable to predators such as malachite kingfishers, which commonly dive for them to feed their young.

The most unusual predators of top-minnows are the fishing spiders. The body of this spider measures only a few centimetres, but it has long slender legs which are well adapted to catching its prey. The rear limbs have small hooks with which it anchors itself to a lily pad or reed. The body and other legs then float motionless, waiting. A passing top-minnow is scooped up by the spider's forelegs and immediately receives a powerful, poisonous and lethal bite. The substances in the bite include a digestive juice, which dissolves the fish's flesh and enables the spider to suck in the juices. The fishing spider can seize a fish up to twice its size, and in the ensuing struggle it may be carried underwater on the back of the fish until the prey finally succumbs.

In the summer the glut of food soon brings a female spider into breeding condition. She does not mate every time, as she can store the sperm from one mating for many months, or even years. She carries the developing eggs on her back in a ball spun with silk, and during this time she does not feed. When the eggs hatch she anchors the ball to a plant and spreads out the silk with her front feet, releasing hundreds of tiny spiders, which she then leaves to fend for themselves. They stay near the ball in their early days, since it acts as a web to catch tiny insects for the spiderlings to eat.

The shallow backwater swamps are important nursery grounds for many fish, and some species spend their entire lives there. The cichlid fish show a wide variety of breeding strategies. One of the most colourful in the Okavango is the jewel cichlid, common in the backwaters where the stems of lilies and reeds provide it with ideal spawning sites. A pair defend their chosen site, and for days after laying and fertilising their eggs they fan water over them to increase the oxygen supply. When hatched the young still depend on the stored food in the yolk sac, and at this stage the female moves them from the spawning site to a clean depression in the sand. She picks them up in her mouth and spits them into the nest, while the male stands by and guards. The young are called 'wrigglers' since they are attached to the sand by threads on their heads, and they wriggle their tails to circulate the water. As they grow they become free-swimming and begin to feed for themselves, but they will remain with their parents for several more weeks as they travel to new, more open areas in search of food.

The banded bream feeds on detritus and algae attached to aquatic plants. Their young develop, and the adults behave, in a similar way to the jewel cichlid. The fanning behaviour of the adults and the 'wriggler' phase in these two fish species are adaptations to the low oxygen levels of the backwater swamps.

Another type of breeding employed by cichlid fish is mouthbrooding. The males of the dwarf mouthbrooder become brightly coloured prior to breeding, as water temperatures increase. A male establishes his territory on the swamp bottom, cleaning and excavating the sand before attracting a female by flashing and shimmering his colours. As she lays the eggs he fertilises them, and then the female takes them into her mouth. The male has marks on his anal fin to attract the female, who bites at them, so taking more sperm from his vent into her mouth and improving the chances of fertilisation. Once the female has all the eggs in her mouth she is chased away by the male, and he plays no further parental role.

The female dwarf mouthbrooder keeps the eggs in her mouth, churning them from time to time to keep them aerated. They hatch after five days, but the young remain in her mouth until they have absorbed their yolk sac and are well developed. The mother cannot feed during this time and her body becomes very thin, while her distended mouth gives her a strange appearance. When the young are released they forage around her and she spits out particles of sand and detritus for them to feed on. She routinely chases off other fish, but if real danger threatens she will signal for them to return to the safety of her mouth.

Mouthbrooding has its benefits in the shallow swamps, where eggs and fry are heavily preyed on by the abundance of aquatic life. This form of protection has its dangers, too, because if the female is caught then so too is her entire family. The striped swamp snake is one likely predator to take a cichlid family. This snake is truly aquatic, a fast agile swimmer, and will ambush prey under water by anchoring itself coiled around an underwater reed. When not hunting it rests in dense vegetation with only the tip of its small head breaking the surface to breathe.

Water lilies cover most of the Okavango's more open water, and when they flower during the hot summer they provide one of the most beautiful sights in the Delta. The blue of the sky is reflected in the sparkling water; the symmetry of tall reeds balances the soft curves of lilies; and the colours of the flowers are bright blues, whites, pale pinks and yellows. In the gusts of wind their upturned leaves flash purple and green. Through the clear water the submerged lily parts can be seen clearly, their stems coiled like springs, their tips bearing small buds of unopened flowers ready to rise above the surface.

There are two main species of water lily in the Okavango. The day-flowering blue lily grows in shallow still waters throughout the Delta, while the yellow night lily occurs in the deeper waters of the channels and around the fringes of larger lagoons. The flowers of the 'blue' lily come in a range of colours, from dark blue to powder blue, pink and white. In contrast to the rather simple design of the yellow night lily the petals and sepals of the blue lily are more finely structured; the smooth edges of the blue lily pads distinguish them from the serrated edges of the night lily pads.

The base of a lily plant consists of a swollen rhizome, eaten as a delicacy, from which numerous spongy roots spread out. The rhizomes give rise to more rhizomes, enabling the plant to reproduce vegetatively. The long stalks of the leaves and flowers contain numerous air canals that keep them afloat and help with the exchange of gases so vital to the plant's respiration and photosynthesis. Groups of calcium oxalate crystals protrude from the walls of the air canals; these are thought to protect the plant from attack by snails and other herbivores. The lily stem continues to grow until the bud is above the surface, where it blossoms. The flower lasts for from four to six days, and during this time the stalk retracts spirally so that the flower is pulled back into the water until it is submerged. Here the fruit ripens and eventually disintegrates, and the tiny red seeds float away in the water.

The blue lily flower usually opens in the morning at about seven o'clock and closes around four in the afternoon. During this time its fragrance and colour attract insects such as flies, beetles and bees, which collect the pollen and nectar. One of the most abundant pollinators is the midge, or gnat, which is sometimes trapped inside the flower as it closes for the night. Midges also lay their eggs inside the lily flower, and these hatch into white larvae. As the flower dies and is pulled below the water, the lack of oxygen makes the midge larvae turn red as they make more haemoglobin, a red oxygen-carrying substance found in blood. This increases their oxygen supply, which they now obtain from the water. The red larvae are called 'bloodworms' and they are a favourite food of the lilytrotter, or African jacana. This bird is well adapted to living in lily lagoons. With its extremely long toes it is able to step lightly from pad to pad as it forages for insects. A jacana pecking at a lily flower is usually feeding on bloodworm larvae.

The jacana's breeding behaviour is most unusual, since it is the male that raises the chicks. The female attracts her mate by beginning to build the nest on a pad of floating vegetation, usually in a lily lagoon. After mating and egg laying, the male incubates the eggs and raises the chicks while the female leaves to look for another mate – who will eventually have to carry out the same parental duties.

When the eggs hatch the male jacana carries away the shells and hides them beneath lily pads, probably so that they do not attract predators. The tiny chicks are 'precocious', able to leave the nest and feed on insects almost at once, although they still look weak and gangling. Initially the male carries the chicks with him as he looks for food, putting them down from time to time to forage for themselves. At the first hint of danger he crouches and calls the chicks to him, encouraging them to climb into his breast feathers. He makes a wonderful sight, stepping cautiously over lily pads with several pairs of stick-like legs protruding from his breast feathers. Sometimes, if suddenly alarmed, the anxious father will accidentally drop the chicks into the water, after which the whole process of crouching, calling and climbing is repeated. After a few days the young are strong enough to follow their father on foraging trips without being carried.

The diminutive pygmy goose also graces the lily lagoons of the Okavango. Here it lives in appreciable numbers, although nowhere is it common. The exquisite colouring and markings of the male – white, bottle green and chestnut – are a perfect camouflage among the brilliant leaves and flowers of a lily lagoon. These geese usually live in pairs, flying fast and low over the water from lagoon to lagoon and resting on the surface as they converse with clear whistling calls.

Pygmy geese feed almost exclusively on lily fruits. When it sees a fruit beneath the surface the goose will dive and peck the stem at a weak point just below the bulb. After several pecks it breaks the fruit free of the stem and the goose can deal further with it at the surface, pecking a hole in the base of the bulb to get out the seeds. During feeding, many seeds are spilled while others are carried away by the current, and yet others are taken by shoals of robber fish and bream which gather expectantly in the vicinity.

Pygmy geese nest in the hollows of old trees or sometimes in the abandoned nests of other birds, such as hammerkops. The female lays up to ten eggs in a down-filled hollow and the goslings leave their nest almost as soon as they hatch; in tree nests they flutter down to the water like the baby goosanders of northern climates. They are able to feed on lily seeds immediately, though at first they depend on the parent to break open the seed pod.

Like many other flowers water lilies have evolved a system to encourage cross-pollination between plants. The male and female parts of the flower ripen at different times. When the flower first opens, the female ovules (seed containers) at the base are ripe but the male stamens do not yet bear pollen, and so a visiting insect which carries pollen from another plant will fertilise the flower. After a day the female parts are no longer receptive and the flower becomes 'male', that is, the stamens start to produce pollen.

The night lily has taken this one step further. It physically traps the visiting insect within its flower, using a device nothing short of murder. During the 'female' stage the base of the flower contains a sticky fluid, above which the male stamens spread in a domed hood. An insect visiting the flower will fly into the hood, slide down the slippery sides of the stamens, and land in the sticky fluid. Smaller insects drown and larger insects are unable to escape from the domed hood, particularly with wet wings. The ensuing struggle ensures that any pollen on the insect falls into the fluid of the female bowl and so fertilises the flower. On subsequent days, when the flower becomes male and bears pollen, the hood of stamens is more open and the fluid dries up. Visiting insects can come and go freely, taking with them pollen to a receptive female flower elsewhere.

The creamy yellow flower of the night lily is one of the most exotic blooms of the Delta. The fact that it blossoms at night suggests that it has some strange and wonderful way of being pollinated, but this has yet to be found. Perhaps the dusk-flying midges are its main pollinators, attracted to the warmth and pungent fragrance of the flower. There are many other mysteries of the night lily; the opening times of its blossoms are also unusual. When a bud first appears above the water it opens at midnight and closes at around eight o'clock the following morning. On the second day the flower opens at nine in the evening and remains open until seven next morning. On the following days it opens at about four in the afternoon and closes at midnight. If there is a reason for this strange pattern of flower opening, the night lily is still guarding one of nature's many mysteries.

CHAPTER SEVEN
ISLANDS OF LIFE

Scattered throughout the Okavango Delta are literally millions of islands. Together, they constitute an area equal to that covered by the Delta's water. In all shapes and sizes, they rise just high enough above the surrounding reedbeds and floodplains to support the growth of trees. Ensured of a regular water supply, the woodlands that fringe the islands grow lofty and luxuriant with species that could otherwise never survive on the impoverished Kalahari sands. The tall yellow-barked sycamore fig, whose leaning fig-laden trunk drops fruit to the fish below, and the densely foliated motsaudi, are two trees that need abundant water at all times.

Sycamore figs line the very edges of the islands, leaning imposingly over the waters of the Delta's lagoons. These elegant trees have an intricate web of life associated with them, in particular with the large fig fruits that grow in heavy branched masses on the trunks and main branches. Clusters of the yellow-red figs ripen often during the year and they are an important food source for the island creatures.

As with all figs, a tiny parasitic wasp is responsible for pollination. The minute female wasp lays her eggs inside the fig fruit by entering the narrow opening at the top of the fruit, called the ostiole. By doing so she pollinates flowers within the fig. The larvae develop as the fruit ripens, and when they are adult they are able to emerge, through a greatly enlarged ostiole. At this stage other, non-pollinating insects such as fruit flies, weevils and beetles are able to enter the fig through this opening, where they lay their eggs in a relatively safe and nutrient-rich environment.

Safe, that is, except for those voracious and abundant little carnivores, the brown ants, which nest in the earth at the bases of fig trees. They raid the ripening figs, taking the wasp larvae and other insects and so they are ensured a regular food supply. Many other creatures enjoy the ripe figs: green pigeons, black-collared barbets, bulbuls, tree rats, baboons and monkeys. By eating the figs they also consume a large number of resident insects – adding protein to the diet. These larger fruit-eaters usually knock some figs off the branches so that they fall into the water below. Fallen figs are taken by many fish, in particular the large purple-headed bream and the red-breasted bream, which build their nests among the half-submerged roots of the fig tree. The smaller robber fish feed on the fig pieces dropped by the bream ... and so the web of life dependent on the figs goes on.

The islands are dazzling in their numbers and variety of form. In the northern permanent swamps they are hillocks so small that there is only room for a single grove of the graceful swamp palm, phoenix. In the seasonal swamps of the middle Delta they become larger, their perimeters edged by a narrow band of woodland comprising an assortment of lovely trees with equally pretty Setswana names – mokutshumo, motsaudi, mokoba, motshaba... Each island is unique in the mix of trees it bears, with its own 'look' and atmosphere.

Towards the southern end of the Delta the islands are quite different. Sometimes called sandveldt tongues, they are extensive areas of Kalahari sand which penetrate deep into the Delta, reminders of the more arid origins of this oasis. The largest, Chief's Island, covers more than 1,000 square kilometres of the central Delta and supports vegetation and animal life more typical of the dry deciduous Kalahari woodlands to the east and north. In the arid interior of Chief's Island, salt pans are interspersed with mopane woodlands and acacia thornscrub, limiting the distribution of the more water-dependent animals. All the larger islands are fringed by a wide margin of floodplain grassland, which is inundated each year by floods only to reappear green and replenished once the waters have passed through.

Most of the smaller islands owe their existence to those ancient and forever active architects and builders, the fungus-growing termites. Their activity not only raises patches of land above the general flatness of the Kalahari but their earth-moving endeavours also enrich the soil, which in turn encourages the growth of trees. Thus termite mounds have their own special web of life, and the tree-filled islands provide the Delta with a diversity of habitats which is reflected in the great variety of birds and animals.

The termite islands, or 'termitaria', also play an important role in the Delta's pattern of water flow, particularly in the seasonal swamps. Termitaria may be built in the narrow entrances to floodplains or in seasonally flooded lagoons. As they grow their bases join together; so the land rises and prevents the flow of water into the formerly flooded area. With time the dried floodplains and 'madiba' (shallow depressions) are colonised by trees, and the work of the termites continues. If several islands are close together the continued activity of the termites will cause the termitaria to join, and a larger island is formed. In this way the lands of the Delta, as well as the waterways, are constantly changing.

It is difficult to be sure when the termite mounds originated. Were some in existence before the Delta formed? If not, how did the termites begin their building activity once the Kalahari sands had flooded? There are currently no firm answers to these mysteries, but since termites as animals evolved well before the delta, many termitaria could have been formed before the Okavango appeared.

There is little doubt that the island-building activities of termites continues. A mound can be constructed by these industrious workers in a very short time, so a temporary change of flow away from an area for one or two seasons could result in the appearance of a mound, which would be the beginning of an island should the waters return again.

Of the 400 termite species in Africa, the fungus termites are the ones responsible for building the large mounds. They cement particles of sand using a mortar of fine clay and saliva as well as calate, a salt found on the edges of the sand islands. The actual shape of a termite mound depends on the species of termite, the local climate and the nature of the soil. Mounds may be ten metres high and shaped as cones, domes or irregular pinnacles. Rain tends to erode the castle-like spires so that an old nest site becomes a grass-covered mound. A healthy termite mound is not static, but continually being enlarged and renewed.

In a typical mound there may be as many termites as there are people in our largest cities. The location of the nest cavity depends on the water table; in the delta they are mostly located high in the mound, well above ground level. The special nest cavity consists of arched clay shelves, on which the fungus gardens grow, and irregular chambers in which the termites live. The huge queen and her consort live in a royal cell in the heart of the mound, where they are constantly attended by workers who carry away the eggs as they are laid. A complex network of corridors leads from the mound into the surrounding countryside, through which termite workers travel in search of wood for food and soil for building.

The ghostly white fungus termites cannot tolerate daylight. They forage at night, or build mud-covered runways at the places where their corridors lead to the surface. They feed on dead wood and animal dung from which they also obtain moisture. It is difficult to appreciate the magnitude of the process. Occasionally an entire tree is covered in mud as, inside, the termites slowly consume it. In this way they remove vast quantities of old wood for recycling. The food is chewed and swallowed by the workers but is only partially digested. The faeces are collected in the mound and used to build the combs on which the fungus gardens grow. The fungi thrive on the partially-digested lignin and cellulose, remnants of the wood in the termites' faeces. They convert their 'food' into nutrients and vitamins that the termites in turn can digest as they crop the fungi. Only one type of fungus is allowed to grow, and it is kept stunted as small spherical growths the size of pin-heads which are fed to the young termites and the royal pair. The fungal beds are carefully tended to provide a constant supply of food for the colony.

By growing fungi, termites can utilise a large variety of substances which would otherwise be inedible.

The termites themselves provide food for a vast range of creatures. Ants appear to be the dominant predators; the African pomerine ant specialises in attacking foraging parties of the worker termites. Lizards, beetles and birds prey heavily on termites, while the list of mammals that take them is very impressive: shrews, vervet monkeys, bushbabies, squirrels, side-striped jackals, genet cats, several species of mongoose and even humans, who relish termites throughout Africa. Other termite predators include scorpions, solifuges (sun spiders), spiders, centipedes, dragonflies, mantids and crickets. There are fewer termite specialists in the Okavango, compared with the more arid grasslands of the Kalahari, perhaps because there is a greater variety of other prey in the Delta. The pangolin is one of the few termite specialists restricted to well-watered areas.

Just after the first rains, winged termites of both sexes leave their nest in a nuptial flight. Their exit from the mound is assisted by the workers, who open up passageways but remain ready to plaster up the holes should predators try and invade. The winged termites, or alates, fly as far as they can before landing. On touchdown the female announces her presence by releasing a pheromone (a scent that acts as a signal) from her waving abdomen. When a male approaches, the couple shed their wings and quickly begin the process of starting a new colony. The fungus termites fly at dusk, when skinks and toads feed on the alates as they approach the surface of the mound, and evening birds and bats swoop over the nests to catch them as they emerge.

As the alates leave their nest the termite workers bring out material from the fungus beds and spread it in the shade near the mound. The fungus develops quickly, producing spores that are then dispersed by the wind. It has been suggested that the termites allow the full development of the fungus from time to time so that the spores will spread, and perhaps new spores from elsewhere will colonise their own material. Presumably such behaviour is instinctive, although one wonders how it originated.

The strong clay termite mounds on the islands provide secure homes among the water and sands of the Okavango Delta. Inside the mounds the networks of galleries, corridors and cavities provide homes for many animal species that are not equipped to dig their own burrows, such as snakes, rodents and lizards. Monitor lizards sometimes lay their eggs in the mounds, carefully covering them with clay-mud afterwards. The eggs incubate, safe and warm, for ten months and then the young hatch out and scratch their way out of the mound – feeding on termites en route.

One of the most unusual residents of termite mounds is the banded rubber frog. It is the only frog which has a neck and this, together with its sticky padded feet, makes it possible for the rubber frog to worm and wriggle its way acrobatically through termitaria corridors in search of its prey. Larger mammals such as the warthog and spotted hyaena often use old and enlarged termitaria hollows as dens for their young.

Yet another creature that takes refuge in termite mounds is the olive grass snake, which hunts its rodent prey among the moist reedbeds and grasses fringing the islands. In the heat of the day this snake likes to 'sunbathe' on the slope of a termite mound. These grass snakes breed towards the end of winter, when a male follows the scent trail of a receptive female. They coil around each other, and mating may take several hours. After a gestation period of two months the female lays about a dozen large white eggs, often in the hollow of a termite mound, where the eggs are well incubated in the warm and moist environment

There are very few prominent river banks or hillocks in the Okavango Delta, and so termite mounds are important nesting sites for birds such as kingfishers. The diminutive jewel-like malachite kingfishers, coloured the greens and blues of the Okavango, commonly excavate their nests in the sides of termitaria. These tiny birds fly like missiles low over the water and are so light that they perch easily on the feathery umbel of a papyrus stem. They have a wonderful 'punk' crest of feathers which is raised when the birds are alarmed or threatened. As the warm weather of summer approaches, from October onwards, the malachites begin to breed. First the male courts the female by feeding her delicate morsels of fish, then together they excavate their nest burrow. The clutch consists of four to six small, white and perfectly round eggs – the eggs of burrowing birds need no camouflage, and they can be round since there is no danger of them rolling out of the nest. Both parents share in the incubation of the eggs and the feeding of the young. While one parent guards the nestlings, the other flies to a nearby backwater to catch top-minnows, juvenile cichlids or reed frogs. On its return the kingfisher perches on a branch near the burrow and announces its presence by a high-pitched call to the mate inside. This bird flies out to begin fishing, and immediately the waiting hunter flies into the termite mound and feeds the chicks. After fledging, the young kingfishers remain with one of the parents so that they can learn to fish. They perch on low reeds and branches that stretch over the water, characteristically bobbing the head and body while waiting for a passing fish. Once the prey is caught it is repeatedly beaten against the perch to kill it.

The presence of islands may partly account for the diversity of bird life in the Okavango Delta. Birds can fly from island to island in search of food and suitable nesting sites, and have a much greater ease of access than land-bound creatures, although elephants, buffaloes, spotted hyaenas and even lions may wade or swim between islands, as they journey through the Delta.

Many of the island trees flower just before the rains. The first is the knobthorn acacia, whose leafless branches, covered by a mass of small white blossoms, provide a lovely sight etched against the blue of the late winter sky. The fragrant flowers attract large numbers of birds and insects, providing them with additional food at the end of winter. The giant stick insect, which feeds on newly emerged catkins, grows to a considerable size – some twenty centimetres long – yet despite this it is well camouflaged against the grey and white bark. The spines on its body even mimic the thorns on the bark of the tree from which the knobthorn gets its name. These thorns develop into thick wooden knobs as the tree matures.

Despite its spiny nature the knobthorn is used by many species. Baboons and squirrels feed on the pods, while tree rats consume the gum which exudes from fissures in the bark. It is perhaps this gum that the elephants are after when they strip the bark. Due to this damage, many trees are susceptible to fire – although even if this kills the trees, they still make useful nesting sites for birds. Woodpeckers and barbets nest in holes inside dead trees, while the scops owl is beautifully camouflaged as it rests by day, motionless, against the trunk.

Palatable grasses grow in their shade, protected from larger herbivores such as hippos by the low thorny branches. The grass seeds provide food for seed-eaters such as fire-finches.

The sausage tree flowers slightly later than the knobthorn acacia, its large burgundy flowers emerging at the same time as the new green leaves. The goblet-shaped flowers are filled with nectar and are visited by insects such as bumble bees and carpenter bees, while the flashing colours of sunbirds shine as they flit from flower to flower. The pungent smell of the sausage tree flowers, which spreads through the warm night air, attracts nectar-feeding bats – which are believed to be one of the tree's main pollinators. The flowers are visited by so many creatures that they usually survive only one day before being knocked to the ground. But their usefulness does not end here, for within the cup-shaped petals collects the dew of dawn, so that creatures like vervet monkeys and tree squirrels can sip moisture from the fallen blossoms.

The sausage-shaped fruits, which give the tree its name, soon develop once the flowers are pollinated. They grow to nearly one metre in length, at which size only larger creatures like elephants, giraffes, hippos and baboons can eat them. Meyer's parrots feed on the seeds embedded deep within the fleshy fruits, patiently removing the pith like taking corn off a cob, until they can remove the seed, crack it open and eat the nutritious kernel.

Of all the trees that fringe the edges of the Delta's islands, the motsaudi offers the deepest and coolest shade. Groves of motsaudi trees are the favourite resting places of elephants during the noonday heat of summer.

The small cream-coloured flowers, which appear briefly before the rains, are almost totally hidden among the dense green foliage. The massed flowers glisten with sweet sticky nectar which, together with their fragrance, attracts many insects. The fruits of the motsaudi ripen with the first rains. Deliciously bitter-sweet, these round orange fruits are relished by many creatures, including monkeys, parrots, squirrels, elephants and man.

A common inhabitant of motsaudi trees is the flap-necked chameleon. This may be because it is about the same size as the leaves and, by taking on the shape and colour of a motsaudi leaf, is easily camouflaged. During the brief flowering period these chameleons feast on the visiting insects, particularly dragonflies that hover to prey on the clouds of midges.

The motsaudi tree lives to a considerable age, and the trunks of the older trees have hollows which deepen with time. These provide safe nesting sites for tree rats, which live throughout the Kalahari in both arid and lush habitats. A nesting mother cuts the leaves of the motsaudi to line her nest in the deep hollow. Should a predator, such as a snake, enter the nest chamber the mother flees – carrying her young, since they remain firmly clasped to her teats. Tree rats are omnivores, feeding at night on motsaudi fruits when in season as well as on the fruits, nuts and shoots of other plants.

The true giant of the island woodlands is the mokutshumo tree, also known as the African ebony, which grows to over 30 metres in height when supplied with limitless water. The sturdy trunk typically forks into two main branches before spreading into a mass of lesser branches and twigs. In time the cleft between the two main boughs becomes eroded by rain, and Pel's fishing owls often raise their chicks in the resulting broad-based hollow. The owls' nest is lined by chippings of bark from the tree and is kept clean by dermestes beetle larvae, which consume the insects attracted to the nest by dropped particles of fish. The female Pel's owl feeds her chick by day, on fish caught by the male at night.

The foliage of the mokutshumo is heavily browsed by elephants. But it is the sweet yellow fruits that cover the tree, usually after most other tree species have fruited, that most animals relish. A fruiting mokutshumo attracts animals from other islands, which crowd round the base of the tree and pick up fruits that have been knocked down by elephants, baboons and fruit-eating birds such as green pigeons. Indeed, the distribution of birds like the green pigeon is largely determined by the distribution of fruiting trees. The dung heaps of the African civet are liberally peppered with mokutshumo seeds, as is the dung of the side-striped jackal. These trees also provide humans with a valuable harvest – San women collect the sweet fruits, which are dried and stored like raisins.

The migratory lesser striped swallows arrive with the summer each year in the Okavango, where they make good use of the island termitaria and trees for breeding. A favourite nest site is the underside of a stout sycamore fig branch, which leans some two metres over the water – presumably a safe place from predators. The bowl-shaped nest is made from moistened clay pellets, which are collected from the edges of termite mounds. The pair work together, taking turns to sit in the half-finished nest while the other collects a beakful of building clay. They build in the mornings only, with a break in the middle for foraging. At dusk large flocks of lesser striped swallows flit and glide over the lagoons as they hunt the evening swarms of midges.

At night the large sycamore fig is once again the site of activity. Fruit bats, of which there are many species in the Delta, leave their dark roosts in the canopies of nearby motsaudi trees to investigate the ripening figs. These bats detect fruit clusters by sight and determine the ripeness by smell, hovering near the figs several times before selecting one. The bat then lands on the fig cluster, grasps the fruit with the two claws on its wings, twists it off, and flies away to a regular roost to feed. In one night a single fruit bat can consume at least twenty of the large sycamore figs. Hanging at the feeding roost by its feet, the bat grasps the fruit in its clawed wings and gradually eats it, each mouthful being slowly chewed to extract the juices. The pips are spat out afterwards, making the bats important agents of seed dispersal. After eating a fig the fruit bat lowers one foot and tilts its body so that it can urinate and defecate without soiling itself. Mother bats carry their babies on feeding forays for the first few weeks, after which they leave the young in the roost, returning at intervals so that the infant bat can lick the fruit juices from its mother's mouth.

Although insect-eating bats locate their prey by the famous 'sonar', using sound waves like radar, the larger fruit bats rely mainly on their highly developed eyesight to locate fruit. Recent research has shown that they have amazingly detailed binocular vision, a result of the structure of the brain as well as their large forward-looking eyes, which can pick up separate images of an object and compare them, to judge depth and distance.

At night the islands come alive with smaller predators on the prowl. Quite at home in the trees is the rusty-spotted genet, a small nocturnal cat-like carnivore that is beautifully camouflaged by its spots, and which balances using its long striped tail. Although related to the mongoose, it is an agile climber and has adaptations that are both feline and canine. Its most common prey are the tree rats that inhabit hollows of old fig and motsaudi trees, though it will hunt a variety of creatures, from insects to small birds, and is quite capable of catching a foraging fruit bat. Unlike its close relative, the small-spotted genet, the rusty-spotted genet is restricted to well-watered areas such as the Okavango Delta. During the day it rests in a tree hollow, where it also raises its litter of young during the breeding season.

Closely related to the genets, but looking quite different, is the African civet. This heavily-set creature more closely resembles a badger than a cat, being twice the length of a genet and five times its weight. It is neither cat nor dog and it is believed that the earliest prehistoric carnivores looked much like it. It is predominantly black in colour, with bold white bars and blotches, and covered in long coarse fur with a thick bushy tail, and a ridge of hair down the back which can be erected into a crest. Like dogs, the civet has non-retractable claws, which more or less confines it to a life on the ground. Despite its large size the civet is a shy nocturnal creature and feeds mainly on fruit and millipedes. The fruit seeds and white millipede casings can be seen in its large dung middens, which are often the only indication of its presence.

A more vocal, and possibly more abundant, predator on the Okavango's islands is the water mongoose. Of all the mongooses it is best suited to well-watered areas, especially along the fringes of swamps and the banks of streams and rivers. A heavily-set creature, it has thick coarse fur which no doubt helps to keep it warm as it swims in cold water at dawn and dusk. These mongooses forage along the edges of the islands and swamps, sometimes in the water and sometimes out. Their long mobile fingers probe in the mud for their prey of frogs, insects and fish. Crabs are their favourite food; they pick these crustaceans out of holes in the shallow banks of the islands. Most prey caught in the water is taken onto dry land to be consumed.

Water mongooses are generally solitary, except when mating which occurs in the winter so that the young are born in the abundance of the summer months. Mating is accompanied by spine-chilling screeches and much spitting and growling, and the courting pair may meet several times in succession, in the same place each night. By day they sleep in the dense reedbeds or in hollows of termitaria.

In the first light of dawn many smaller creatures move through the reeds that mark the boundary between the islands and the backwater swamps. Moss-covered pathways weave their way through a canopy of fallen matted grasses and sedges, following the water's edge. These paths mark the foraging routes of swamp rodents such as the semi-aquatic, web-footed swamp rat, which feeds on the roots and shoots of swamp vegetation as well as the seed heads of sedges. Musk shrews, being smaller and lighter, use the established pathways of swamp rats. Being insectivorous, the shrews do not compete with the herbivorous rats.

Musk shrews, like shrews in general, are primitive creatures. The first mammals on earth, some 200 million years ago, were probably shrew-like. Their eyes are tiny, their eyesight poor, and they rely on long snouts and a faceful of whiskers sensitive to the vibrations set up by their moving prey. The body is low and wedge-shaped, adapted to foraging in thick vegetation. The large, insect-crushing incisor teeth make drinking difficult, so the animal drinks by dipping its mouth in water and then raising its head and letting the liquid trickle down its throat. The shrew's high metabolic rate means it burns up energy fast, so it must feed frequently and for most of the day and night. When not out and about these animals rest in burrows in the moss-covered ground. The glands on the flanks of both sexes give the musk shrews their name and their characteristic smell when alarmed. The heavy musk odour also taints the flesh and so they are seldom preyed on, except by owls, and most probably by the group-living, ground-dwelling marsh owls.

The so-called tiny musk shrew is probably the smallest mammal in the Okavango, weighing only six grams. However, this opportunistic hunter needs nearly that weight of insects a day to keep it going. One easy way to obtain a dragonfly nearly its own length is to steal one from the sticky trap of the carnivorous swamp plant, the sundew.

The larger lagoons of the central delta, of which the Gedikwe Lagoon is one of the biggest and most famous, contain a somewhat different type of island. This is the tree island of the water fig, or gomoti fig, which grows in thickets in the shallow water, often making a tangle of stems and branches. It produces shady thickets under which rest hippos and crocodiles. Like all figs, the trees of these islands provide important food. The tiny red berries are taken by fruit-eating birds such as colourful and noisy crested barbets, pigeons, doves, grey louries and parrots. Figs that are knocked into the water are taken by fish. The leaves are eaten by elephants and sitatungas. But probably the most important role of the gomoti islands in the Okavango is as breeding colonies for numerous species of birds.

Yellow-billed and open-billed storks, several species of heron, marabou storks and ibises nest in the water figs. As many as twenty-four species have been recorded breeding on the islands in Gedikwe Lagoon, in the heart of the Delta. Although situated in deep water, a land base has built up beneath and around the trees from centuries of bird droppings and the deposition of sediments and general detritus which collect around the submerged root-masses. The birds begin to congregate on the islands in winter, so that most nest building and egg laying is completed before the rains. Species with longer incubation times such as marabou storks and yellow-billed storks begin their nest building and mating displays first. There is a frenzy of building activity as the birds gather grasses, leaves and twigs from communal collecting areas on the islands close to the fig colony. Breeding seems to be timed so that most chicks hatch out in November, when the water level is at its lowest and therefore the fish prey are at their highest densities – which greatly assists the parents in feeding their young.

The large number and variety of breeding birds is made possible by the densely tangled nature of the water figs. Different birds nest at different heights. Smaller and more vulnerable species such as purple herons and sacred ibises nest in the dense lower parts of the trees, which offer shade and greater protection. Larger birds such as marabou storks and yellow-billed storks construct nests on the canopy of the water fig – perhaps their larger body size makes it easier to cover and cool their eggs and to protect the chicks from raptors (birds of prey) such as kites and tawny eagles.

One of the great advantages of breeding on fig islands is that few of the land-based egg and chick predators can invade the colony. However against the large handsome Nile monitor there is little protection. These lizards swim like otters and are beautifully camouflaged in the swampy waters with a glistening skin of mottled greens and yellows. The Nile monitor has no problem moving over and through the tangled fig trees with the aid of its strong sharp claws, in search of eggs and young nestlings.

The intense heat can be a problem, particularly for the birds nesting in the upper levels of the fig colony. Behaviour for cooling the eggs includes shading them with body and outstretched wings, or sitting on the eggs with wet feathers. Eggs are also wetted, and so cooled, by the parents defecating on them, regurgitating water over them, or sometimes dragging wet weeds over them. When the birds need to drink or collect water they regularly use a special pool close to the nesting area.

Open-billed storks are comic-looking birds with an open section midway down the bill, with which they are able to crack open their favourite prey of mussels and snails. With such a specialised adaptation they often travel far to feed, perhaps more than a hundred kilometres, since mussels and snails grow mainly on the submerged rhizomes of papyrus, deep in the murky reed swamps. The birds follow areas of fire damage through the Delta, where the surface vegetation has burned away and they can more easily find their prey. When a group leaves the colony the storks circle above the fig islands to catch a thermal, which carries them high in the sky and assists them in covering the long distances to their feeding grounds. The Delta is truly the domain of those creatures that can fly, over reedbeds, swamplands and lagoons, from island to island.

CHAPTER EIGHT
PASTURES OF THE FLOOD

As the Okavango Delta stretches and spreads through its lower reaches, the perennial reedbeds and swamps give way to seasonal swamps and large tracts of grasslands. These are in turn increasingly interspersed by large islands of sand and sandveldt tongues. The grassed plains, called floodplains, owe their existence to the seasonal inundation from the floods and the rains. The land is wet enough to prevent colonisation by woodlands, but receives too little water to support the rank lush growth of reedbeds. The floodplain grasslands are of great importance to the larger grazing mammals of northern Botswana and it is here, where the Kalahari meets the Delta, that the vegetation and wildlife are at their most diverse.

The most abundant large mammal of the floodplain grasslands is the semi-aquatic antelope, the red lechwe. It occurs in large numbers throughout the delta, and this is its southernmost distribution in Africa. It is essentially a swamp antelope, though not quite as specialised as the sitatunga, which lives in much denser reedbeds. The red lechwe prefers the borders between swamps and grasslands, where it grazes on the young shoots of sedges and grasses growing in the shallow waters. A common sight in the Okavango is a small group of red lechwes bounding in their characteristic loping gait through the shallow waters of the floodplains, sending up sprays of water that sparkle in the sun.

The preference of red lechwes for shallow waters has as much to do with their physical adaptations as with their need to feed on green grasses. They have elongated hooves for moving through thick reedbeds and soft mud; together with their bounding gait, the hooves make it possible for lechwes to run faster through shallow water than on dry land. When alarmed they readily take to water, and their speed gives them a great advantage against their main predators – lions, leopards, wild dogs and humans. However, lechwes are particularly vulnerable when the floodplains are dry, and so they tend to move with the water. During high floods they move ahead of the waters, from the more permanent swamps onto the grasslands, and then they retreat again as the floods subside.

The breeding season of the red lechwe is also timed to coincide with the seasonal flooding pattern in the Delta. The main mating period is during the rains, from January to April, so that the young are born just after the floods recede in September, leaving the floodplains green and lush with food. Only adult male lechwes that hold territories can mate with females; the latter live in herds of twenty or so with their young. These female herds are relatively independent and move from territory to territory as they choose, attracted by areas of better grazing. It is important for a male to hold one of the better territories and there is much competition, with fighting and displaying, to establish dominance. The strongest males hold the best territories, have the most access to female groups, and so pass on their genes in the classic style of natural selection. The favoured territories (about four hectares in size) are along stretches of open water on the floodplains, so that there is access to both habitats. By day the lechwes rest on termite mounds, which act as good lookout points, while at night they sleep away from the water's edge, probably to avoid crocodiles. On the alert, a proud male lechwe surveys his territory from the elevation of a termite mound, his heavy chestnut coat a perfect foil to the tawny grass and silver-red miscanthus flowers.

The floodplain communities form a mosaic through the Delta, depending on the pattern of flooding and the occurrence of sand islands and termite mounds. The seasonally inundated swamps are the first areas to receive water in times of heavy rains or floods; if the floods are particularly high they receive water throughout the year. Because of the regular flooding, the dominant plants are sedges and water-tolerant grasses. Although the vegetation looks temptingly green and lush, the sedges are similar to papyrus in their coarseness and lack of nutrients and protein. Even so, they are important to red lechwes.

As the grasslands dry out the lechwes move with the receding water level, and reedbucks move into the area instead. These shy antelopes live in thick vegetation in pairs or family parties, always near water. When a reedbuck sees a potential predator it often hides behind a clump of reeds, ducking its head low but with its hindquarters showing clearly. There can be few better examples of 'playing ostrich'! In the driest conditions the large herbivores move in, including buffaloes, zebras, wildebeests and impalas, probably because their other grasslands have become overgrazed and they need to be closer to the ever-receding waters of the Delta.

The grasslands occur on sandy soils and are the last areas of the Delta to be flooded. Again, there is a mosaic of floodplain communities – short grass, long grass, shrubs and bushes. These secondary grasslands are typically backed by the woodlands of the northern Kalahari interior, so that as the inland pans dry out, more and more grazing animals return to the Delta for water. At times as many as twenty species of large herbivores use the dry floodplains, so the arrival of the floods is important in protecting the grasses from overgrazing. Adjacent to most islands, and often enclosed by riverside woodlands or termite islands, are small patches of short grasses and sedges which are also covered only during the floods. These areas are used by lechwes and also by hippos which come out of the water to graze on the grasses.

Hippos are important agents of 'nutrient transfer', for they graze on land and defecate in the water. Generally they graze at night, spending the hot days lolling in the cool waters. Territorial male hippos frequently spray dung on their land-based territories, too, and this is the base of another important cycle of nutrients. Fungus termites build their mounds throughout the floodplains and this produces richer soils as the mounds are worn down by wind, rain and floods. The bases of the mounds become stabilised by shorter, more nutritious grasses which are the food of the harvester termites – those grass-processing insects so important in the Kalahari sandveldt. The harvester termites also collect and process the sprays of hippo dung, since these contain undigested fragments of their preferred grasses. In this way there is a close link between the hippos, mound-building fungus termites and harvester termites, each contributing to the enrichment of the floodplain soils.

The impala and the tsessebe (or topi) are found on the floodplains throughout the year. They are relatively stationary, not following the pattern of flooding like lechwe, nor dispersing into the sand islands and sandveldt tongues like buffaloes and zebras. Tsessebes inhabit the floodplain grasses for, unlike their close relative the red hartebeest, they are dependent on water. The males live in permanent territories on the floodplains and do not wander into the Kalahari interior during the rains. Tsessebes have an almost clown-like appearance, with the comical face of the hartebeest and sloping hindquarters, and yet they are remarkably fast and agile – perhaps the fastest of all antelopes. They are seldom killed by lions, although they have less resistance against the efficiency of pack-hunting wild dogs.

Impalas are common in the Delta and are frequently seen grazing on the floodplains or disappearing into the dappled shade of the mopane woodlands during the heat of day. Their abundance is no doubt related to the amount of their preferred habitat, the 'edge' areas between open grasslands and wood and bushland, since they are both grazers of grass and browsers of bushes. They are a highly evolved antelope, being a gregarious species with feeding habits that enable them to occur in large numbers and high densities, since they feed on different plants as these become available. In the Okavango impalas rut in May, so most calves are born after the annual floods have receded and when new grasses are exposed on the floodplains.

Antelopes living in open habitats, such as springboks, use visual signals for communication and have conspicuous coat patterns. The impala, however, is suited to a slightly denser habitat such as open woodlands, and vocal signals are more important. During the mating season in winter, there is much roaring amongst territorial males.

Scent is another means of communication. Impalas have scent glands on their foreheads, and the rubbing of bushes by males is important in defining their otherwise loosely marked territories. Another unique feature of impalas, related both to their gregariousness and to their movements in denser habitats, is that both sexes possess large scent glands on their heels. The scent is probably important in laying a trail which enables individuals to keep in contact in the woodlands, where visibility is poor. One of the Okavango's thrilling sights is of impalas leaping spectacularly and bounding from side to side as they scatter through bushes when alarmed. It has been suggested that this characteristic jumping has a function beyond simply confusing a pursuing predator. Despite the apparently random leaping of animals from side to side, the momentum of the leaps quickly establishes a general direction of flight for the herd, and the tendency to leap this way and that seems to retain contact between the group, despite the often thick bush, by means of the fetlock gland present on all the animals. As the impalas leap they kick out their heels, which seems to cause the fetlock gland to expand. It is possible that a puff of scent is released into the air, leaving a trail which is easier for running animals to follow than a scent trail on the ground. Despite this group cohesion, impalas are frequently taken by predators including lions, spotted hyaenas, leopards, cheetahs and wild dogs – although a large proportion of kills are of solitary animals. Juvenile impalas are preyed on by jackals, the smaller cats, baboons, eagles and pythons.

Large herds of Cape buffaloes are found in the Delta throughout the year. There is a resident population of about 20,000 animals, which does not include dry-season migrants from the Kalahari woodlands farther north. The resident buffaloes prefer to inhabit the interiors of the sand islands such as Chief's Island, where they obtain water from rain-filled pans. Their preference for the grasses of the sandy areas highlights the fact that, despite looking thick and luxuriant, the floodplain grasses are coarse and low in protein. The abundance of water encourages fast growth but provides little substance. The nitrogen-returning properties of some acacia trees in the more arid sandy areas helps to encourage the growth of sweeter, albeit less dense and tall, grasses.

It is possible for buffaloes to graze in the sand islands and sandveldt tongues only during the rains, when the pans hold water. This seasonal availability of good grazing is responsible for their narrow and high birth 'peak' from January to March, during the rains. Towards the end of the dry season they leave the sand masses and large concentrations roam the mosaic of islands and floodplains in the seasonal swamps. The dry-season change to floodplain grasses, and the large numbers of animals on relatively small areas, cause the buffaloes to lose up to a quarter of their total body weight.

The palm groves of the sandy islands have their own special sounds as the leaves rustle and scrape in the wind. High on the top of the tallest palm tree is a large nest of dry branches. A white-backed vulture circles overhead and lands on its eyrie to feed its chick. Hyphaene palms tower overhead, their fan-shaped leaves etched against the blue sky; half hidden in the thick fronds are massive clusters of large shiny ginger-coloured fruits. Filtered sunlight reflects on the white sands sparsely covered by spiky grasses. The palm grove here might seem like an extension of the famous palm belt of the Makgadikgadi Pan, deep in the Kalahari; in fact it is one of many palm groves scattered on the sandier islands and sandveldt tongues of the central and lower delta. These ridges of Kalahari sand, which raise the land high above the transforming effects of water, retain many of the characteristics of the arid Kalahari, including the animals more typical of its grasslands and woodlands. There is only one difference – within a short walk is an abundance of clear fresh water.

Only the fringes of the sand islands, some of which are several thousand square kilometres in size, are affected by the flooding regime, which leaves a narrow band of floodplain grasses along its edges. It is surprising to see the grasses and sedges of these narrow floodplains covered with a white powder, like a gentle snowfall. The powder is in fact a mass of salt crystals (sodium bicarbonate) brought in with the waters of the Okavango. The crystals form as the water evaporates. A by-product of this process, called calate, is a material used by termites to build their mounds. In the perennial swamps the salts are continually flushed away, but they accumulate on the sand islands since it is here that most of the Delta's evaporation occurs. This is the same process that created the salt pans of the Middle Kalahari but here, in the Delta, the annual cycle of floods and rains combines to wash the crystals away each year. Few grasses can tolerate the salinity of these areas. The couch grass, a remarkable African species, is one of them. A limited number of creatures has also made use of this specialised habitat, including the funnel-web spider, whose white web is spread out between the salt-covered grass stems. The spider waits in its camouflaged silk-lined tunnel until a fly or midge falls into the trap. The insect is immediately pounced on and consumed.

A few metres inland the sands rise enough to avoid flooding, but the water-table is still high enough to support woodlands of knobthorn and combretum trees. *Hyphaene* palm groves occur in areas where the underground waters tend towards brackishness – in particular at the flooded saline edges of sand islands. The tracks in the loose white sands tell of the many creatures that move through the dryland woods and down to the water's edge to drink. The large round prints of elephants; the different shapes and sizes of the cloven-hoofed animals such as giraffes, kudus, impalas, buffaloes and warthogs; and the pug marks which tell of the presence of nocturnal carnivores such as hyaenas, lions, leopards and the small side-striped jackals.

The *Hyphaene* palm groves are frequented by elephants. The fronds of those trees within reach of an elephant's trunk have brown jagged edges where the leaves have been chewed off. The topmost bud of a seedling palm is delicious – but it is well protected against browsing with tough spikes. Elephants are passionately fond of the palm fruits and move from island to island in search of fruiting trees. Despite the impressive heights of some palms, an adult elephant can easily wrap its trunk round the stem and shake the tree vigorously to dislodge the fruits. Chacma baboons also like the sweet ginger-flavoured pith of the *Hyphaene* fruit, and they often feed in the wake of elephants, making use of those fruits the elephants have shaken loose but not eaten.

The *Hyphaene* palm fruits are the size of large apples but weigh considerably more. On average a tree bears about fifty kilograms of fruits. The hard shiny brown shell covers a thin layer of edible flesh which encloses a hard bony kernel of 'vegetable ivory'. The weight of the fruit restricts its dispersal to the two main agents mentioned – elephants and baboons. Otherwise it is far too big and heavy to be carried by birds or small mammals. Baboons may carry a fruit a short distance, probably to prevent it being stolen by another baboon, to be eaten on a nearby perch. Here the seed in the kernel is dropped. Only the elephant is large enough for the long-distance dispersal of the seeds. It is often believed that the *Hyphaene* seed must pass through the gut of an elephant before it can germinate. This is not true, although the seedling obviously benefits from a start to life in a large moist dung heap. It is more likely that fire is an important stimulus for germination. Indeed fires are common in the dry season on these islands. The adult palms are well adapted to withstand them since they do not have bark to damage; the full diameter of the stem develops underground. The occurrence of pure groves of these palms may be related to fire, since other trees would be destroyed.

Hyphaene palms have a curious bulge mid-way down the grey fluted stem. Research so far indicates that the bulge is not related to the tree's water economy, nor is it for strength in the tall stem. It has been suggested that the bulge evolved to prevent monkeys from climbing the stem and robbing the fruits before they are ripe. Although a tempting hypothesis it is not true, since chacma baboons easily shin up and down the stems and the wide-based crowns are their favourite nesting places at night! Many creatures use the dense crowns for nesting, including buffalo weaver birds, who build large communal nests which are used by tree rats once the birds leave. *Hyphaene* palms are also used as roosts by bats. One of the great attractions of this palm's crown is the tree's tendency to retain the large fronds for a long time after they have died. The dead leaves form massive clusters which provide cover and shade for many creatures. In return the nesting creatures defecate or drop food at the base of the palm, thus adding to the nutrients of the soil.

Leaving the edges of the sand islands, the vegetation becomes truly dry-land in nature. On the sandier soils the camelthorn acacia replaces the knobthorn acacia, while the woodlands are interspersed by combretum and silver terminalia trees on very deep sands. Where the soils contain more clay the mopane woodlands grow. Elephants love to feed on the seed and leaves, and especially the roots, of terminalia, although these trees grow in areas of deep sand, which restricts their use by elephants except in the middle of the rains. These dry interior woodlands support the growth of sweet grasses, as well as tasty shrubs and herbs. The grewia bushes in particular have nutritious leaves and an abundance of small, brown and very sweet berries. The woodlands are populated by elephants, buffaloes, zebras, wildebeests, giraffes and kudus, especially in the rains when the short grasses are green, the trees have a flush of new leaves, and the water pans are full. As the dry season advances and the pans dry out the animals gradually drift back to the floodplains where they are closer to water.

Before the large animals return, whether from the sand islands or the Kalahari interior, the floodplains are relatively empty. Interesting associations between animals are at their most evident. The wattled crane feeds in shallow water, often in association with lechwes. With its large bill it digs up the roots of the grasses and sedges that lechwes feed on. These large elegant birds are migratory, flying to remote wetlands where they feed and breed undisturbed. Of the four species of cranes in Africa, the wattled crane is the most dependent on water; it is also the rarest. The Okavango Delta is one of the most important breeding grounds for this species in the world, since it requires large undisturbed territories, to ensure sufficient food and as security against predators. During their moult in spring the cranes cannot fly, so they are particularly vulnerable to disturbance and predation. A pair needs an area of roughly 30 hectares to nest, with 150 hectares of surrounding floodplain grassland in which to feed. The non-breeding birds form highly nomadic flocks.

With the rains long since gone, and winter approaching, many of the floodplains are dry. The grasses are tall and coarse, and the ground hard, awaiting the floods. On the drying grasslands chacma baboons and warthogs forage together. Warthogs are expert diggers, rooting up the more nutritious tubers of plants and lilies that the receding waters have exposed. The males of the baboon troops are notoriously vigilant, with large males defending the females and young in their troop from predators. Probably for this reason the warthogs tolerate the baboons nearby. They benefit from the advance warning of danger, and in turn the baboons have a share of the warthogs' rooting and digging.

The low waters create unusually high concentrations of fish in the shallow pools fringing the floodplains. The thin-faced bream is a predatory cichlid specialised for hunting in these densely reeded areas, partly on account of its long thin body and snout. It lurks camouflaged behind reeds, remaining motionless for long periods until an unwary fish approaches within striking distance. Suddenly the bream lunges forward, protrudes its jaws into a cone and sucks in the fish.

Another fish specialist of the floodplains is the climbing perch. It has accessory breathing organs in the gills which enable it to live in the oxygen-deficient waters of shallow pools and swamps. As the pools of the drying floodplains become smaller and smaller, so the stranded climbing perch finds itself short of water and food. But it is able to move short distances overland to a new pool, 'walking' by lying on its side and pulling itself along using the serrated edge of its gill flap. It is a wonder just how it determines the location of a nearby pool. Climbing perches are well camouflaged, presumably to avoid predation from birds as they move overland.

As May turns into June the winter sets in and brings with it the dry season. The changes in the Okavango Delta are more subtle than those of the Kalahari, for the presence of water and vegetation tempers the cold and aridity. At night the cool clear skies are laden with stars; buffaloes and lechwes move onto the islands to seek warmth beneath the big trees. On the islands nocturnal predators search for their much diminished prey. Snakes, frogs and musk shrews have gone into semi-hibernation; however tree rats still abound and are probably the major prey of small carnivores at this time. In the narrow reed-lined channels little bee-eaters crowd together along a slender reed overhanging the water, huddled close to keep out the night's chill. Occasionally the entire line is disturbed as the end bird flies up and tries to squeeze into the cosy middle. Although little bee-eaters form territorial breeding pairs in summer, in the winter they are found at night in larger groups, probably to keep warm.

Despite the cloudless skies, the chill of morning is burnt off only around noon. Life, both plant and animal, seems to have paused – as if in suspense, waiting until the warmth and rain bring renewed activity. On the islands there are no trees in fruit or flower, with one important exception, the winter-flowering mistletoe that grows on the knobthorn trees. The delicate blossoms of the mistletoe are an important source of nectar in the dry season and are frequented by birds, carpenter bees, honey bees and ants. The jewel colours of sunbirds such as Marico's sunbird, the white-bellied sunbird and the collared sunbird flash from flower to flower as they feed on nectar and the occasional ant. The ripe berries of the mistletoes are taken by frugivorous (fruit-eating) birds such as the spectacularly coloured crested barbets. The birds wipe the sticky seeds off their beaks onto the bark of trees, and here some of the seeds will germinate and new plants grow. It is a mystery as to why acacias are generally the preferred host of the parasitic mistletoe. It might be because the dense thorny branches of the acacia protect the mistletoe from browsing animals.

The mistletoe is host to several species of caterpillars. It is common to see at least two types feeding on the plant, each using different survival strategies. The gregarious dotted border caterpillar depends on its striking coloration and hairy appearance to warn potential predators of its distastefulness, so that it can feed openly. These larvae emerge from their eggs together, feed and move from leaf to leaf in a caravan, and also pupate (become chrysalises) together – all tactics for safety in numbers.

The caterpillar of the pretty short-barred sapphire butterfly uses a very different strategy. It mimics any portion of the mistletoe plant it happens to feed on. The larva is orange when feeding on the flower; as it moves onto a leaf it takes on a silvery-green coloration, with its head looking like the nibbled edge of the leaf. It pupates on the grey stem of the mistletoe, where it resembles a bird dropping. This type of protective mimicry means that the larva is safest alone, and it moves almost imperceptibly as it feeds.

The short-barred sapphire is a member of the lycaenid group of butterflies, fascinating not only because they are highly specific to their food plant but also because they have evolved a life-cycle which makes use of those abundant little predators, the ants. The majority of lycaenid caterpillars are 'milked' by ants, which rub a honey-gland on the back of the larva so that it exudes drops of honey-dew. In turn the ants protect the caterpillars, in many cases taking them off their food plant and carrying them into their nest. Here the caterpillars are protected from the ravages of grass fires, or from birds and other predators. Butterflies, after emerging from the pupae, make a quick exit from the ants' nest before their wings begin to expand.

In the winter lagoons the water is an icy blue, a mirror to the immense cloudless skies. The flowers of the water lilies have died back with the cold, and the papyrus stands tall and lifeless. In the glassy channels the only flowers are the delicate white blossoms of ottelia, which look like snowdrops on an ice-covered meadow. The aquatic ottelia has stems covered by spiky bumps and a thin layer of mucus, which may help to prevent fish from eating them. The fragile blossoms are supported on a single air bladder which keeps them above the water, ready to be pollinated by insects. The waters are too cold for fish to breed, and this must be a lean time for aquatic predators.

On the floodplains in winter the grasses are dry and coarse. Despite this an inexorable movement of large mammals occurs, leaving the dry interior of the Kalahari and the Delta's sand masses to begin their concentration on the drying floodplains – despite the low quality of the grazing. During the dry season there is a tenfold increase in buffaloes, zebras and elephants in the Delta. The large predators arrive in their wake, and for them it is a season of plenty. The most water-dependent herbivores arrive first. Large herds of zebras and buffaloes congregate on the floodplains; elephants and sable antelopes emerge from the mopane woodlands as the last water pans dry out. There are grazing differences among the herbivores whereby the larger animals such as buffaloes and zebras (which can tolerate the coarsest vegetation) feed on the tallest and least palatable grasses. This makes the shorter, more nutritious grass available to more selective feeders such as sables, wildebeests and tsessebes. They in turn graze the grass to the short length preferred by steenboks, impalas and warthogs. In this way a large number and variety of grazing animals can co-exist with less competition than if they all had similar food preferences.

On the dry brown floodplains there is now a sense of expectancy, despite being in the depths of the cold and rainless winter season. Soon an amazing event will occur, bringing new life to the Delta's southerly grasslands. The floods are coming from the north.

CHAPTER NINE
FLOOD-TIDE

In Botswana the word for rain is 'pula', the name also given to the nation's currency. Such is the value placed on this precious resource in the Kalahari. The rains fall mainly in the hot season from November to March, but the pattern constantly changes. In some years there is almost no rain, so that drought conditions prevail. Large continental air masses bring with them high atmospheric pressure, heat, wind and clouds, and – sometimes – the rains. The Okavango Delta always has more rain than the arid parts of the Kalahari. No doubt the Delta's water and the swamp vegetation create their own local climate, much as tropical rain forests do. Although rain provides a third of the Delta's water, it is all lost by evaporation. The build-up to rain lasts many months. Most of this time the dark skies, high winds and heavy oppressive heat (that high-pressure heat which comes from being in the very heart of a massive continent) produce nothing but storms of sand.

Scattered storm clouds and isolated showers are the characteristic form of rain over the Delta. Size, however, is deceptive. An isolated storm that appears small in the vastness of the Delta may, in fact, measure eighty kilometres across. Its immense power is apparent in the blackness of the storm clouds. The heavy summer atmosphere builds slowly; the oppressive heat and hot winds are the first announcements. Storm clouds, at first so distant, move across the sky, a gunmetal grey with their leading edges tinged gold by the rays of a sun which will soon be obliterated. The wind howls and swirls; the tall grass crackles, rustles and whispers as it is stirred by the hot air that swirls beneath the darkening sky. In the far distance another isolated storm moves across the horizon. The clouds now race overhead; lightning flashes and thunder rumbles in their approaching black heart. In the distance the rain is white. Leaves are torn from the trees and carried high by the winds, which continue to gain momentum. White egrets shimmer against the slate-grey clouds, the birds being tossed about like the wind-torn leaves. Suddenly there is a lull, and the rain falls. As the clouds move on the rain-washed landscape receives the sun's rays again and a rainbow shimmers in the distance. The storm passes and before long the air is hot again.

The rains raise the level of water here and there in the Delta, but their impact is small in comparison with another rain-borne event that occurs

Opposite: The Delta's islands (top), dazzling in variety and number, are visited by large animals which cut paths through the shallow water. A male olive grass snake (bottom) finds a receptive female by following her scent trail.

each year – the floods. The rainfall in the highlands of Angola is considerably higher than in Botswana. Rainwater collects within this huge catchment and is channelled down the Okavango River, swelling its banks and producing a flood-tide of water which gradually arrives at the Delta. In the upper reaches of the Delta the river reaches a peak height in February or March, and so the Panhandle is the only area to receive the floods at the same time as the rains. As the flood travels down the river bed of the Panhandle it overflows its banks, revitalising the swamps and covering the sandbanks. On reaching the fan-shaped Delta it spreads out, overflowing river channels and the banks between clumps of reeds and papyrus, inundating floodplains and slowly raising the water level in lagoons and backwaters. The flood's front moves slowly, travelling at speeds rarely exceeding one kilometre a day – partly due to the flatness of the terrain, and partly because the water is slowed by the swamp vegetation. At this speed the floods take some five months to travel the length of the Delta, arriving in the southern floodplains in the midst of the dry season. Here it is a flood of new life.

The dramatic change that the annual floods bring to the Delta is first felt in the Panhandle. The papyrus swamps, which have become increasingly dry, are now flushed with fresh water. Most of the swamp inhabitants breed at this time because the oxygen level in the water rises with the rain and floods. The sitatungas have their calves, moving out into the previously inaccessible swamplands where there is plenty of food and cover. The rising waters slowly cover the sandbanks. The African skimmer chicks have already fledged, and the last few skimmers leave their summer breeding grounds to travel north again. They will not return to grace the sunset waters of the Okavango River until the following September. The crocodiles' eggs also hatch before their sandbank nests are covered by the flood. The rising water level forms new pools in the swamplands beyond the main river, where the young crocodiles are safer, and where their insect food is more plentiful.

The barbels that have swum northwards, like packs of hunting dogs, find their breeding grounds. They move into the shallows of the floodplains to spawn in large numbers. There is apparently a great urgency to spawn at the start of the floods, in water so shallow that the fish can barely swim. This may be an evolutionary mechanism to guarantee a continuous current that flushes and oxygenates the eggs. The fishermen of the Panhandle have learned of this temporary abundance of easily-caught fish. They wade out into the shallows to spear the large barbel as they move relentlessly to their spawning grounds.

In the swamps and reedbeds of the Okavango the seasonal floods distribute the 'old water', which is enriched with the organic matter, sludge and detritus which has accumulated in the swamps between floods. Thus the flood regime has important effects throughout the Delta. It enriches the

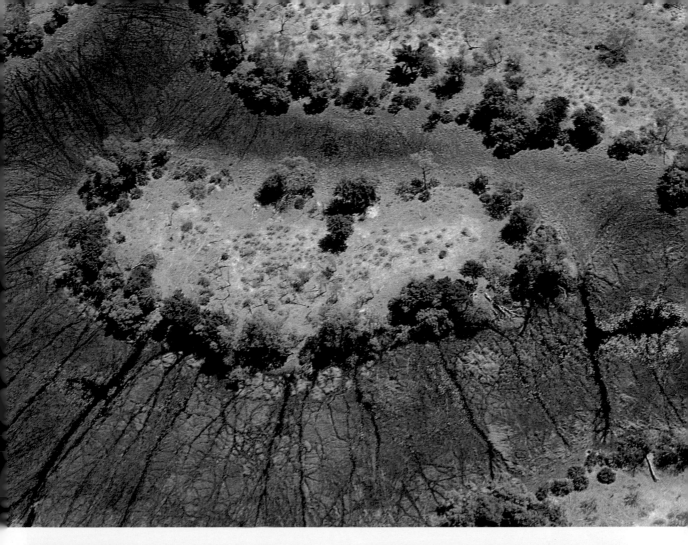

Many islands exist because of termite mounds (opposite), which raise the level of the land above the water. At night the rusty spotted genet (below) waits in ambush in a tree, while the semi-aquatic marsh mongoose (bottom) forages along the edges of islands.
Overleaf: Large areas of grassland are flooded each year.

Impalas are both browsers and grazers, and are abundant in the transitional habitat between grasslands and woodland which fringe the islands and land masses of the Okavango Delta.

The semi-aquatic red lechwe (below) usually runs through shallow water to escape potential predators. Together with the chacma baboon (bottom), they are the most numerous mammals of the Delta. In the dry season, Cape buffalo concentrate in large herds on the floodplains (opposite).

186

New grasses sprout from the flooded winter grasslands (below).
The winter-flowering mistletoe is browsed by dotted border caterpillars
(bottom) which feed and pupate together as a tactic against predation.
On winter's nights, little bee-eaters huddle together for warmth
(opposite).

In the cold dry season elephants return from the Kalahari interior to the waters of the north and west (below), and hippos (opposite top) bask after the winter chill of early morning. The palm islands of the Lower Delta (opposite bottom), reminiscent of Makgadikgadi's palm belt, are isolated by the floods.

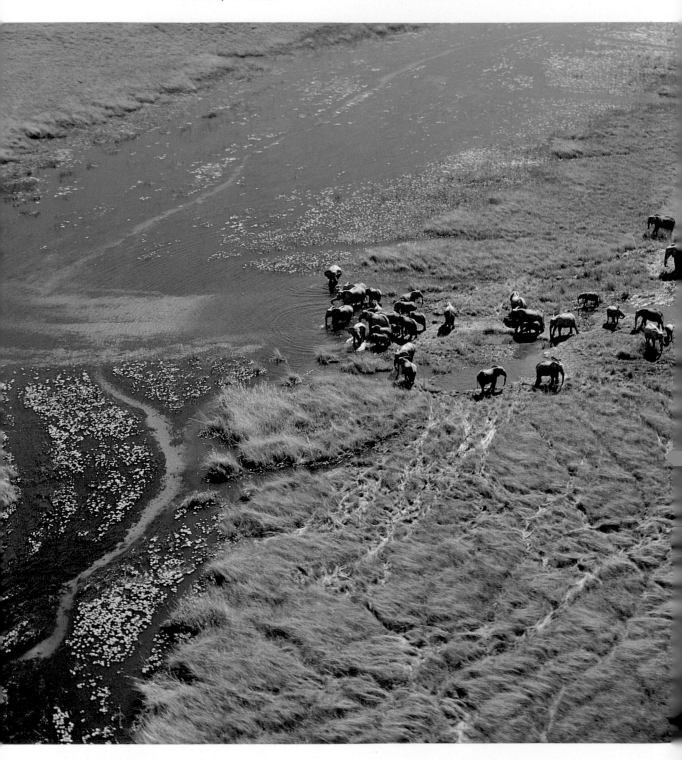

The wild dog (opposite) is highly social, living and hunting in packs. Males remain in their pack of birth, while females over two years join unrelated packs. Africa's largest stork, the saddle-bill (below), flies to floodplain grasslands to feed on fish brought in by the flood.

Opposite: In the dry season the annual flood, having journeyed for five months from the rain-fed rivers of Angola, spills and spreads over the dry floodplains of the Lower Delta.

lower regions with regular supplies of silt and detritus, as well as providing water to sustain the seasonal swamps and floodplains. Slowly the floodwaters filter and trickle through the endless reedbeds, raising the level around the sand islands and causing water to evaporate, leaving salt deposits on the sandy surface.

In the northern seasonal swamps and lagoons the water level rises slowly, almost imperceptibly. The floods bring with them many subtle changes in these lagoons and reedbeds. Coiled lily stems untwist to compensate for the increase in the water's depth. The burrows of semi-aquatic rodents and shrews are flooded by the rising waters and have to be evacuated. The floods here arrive towards the end of the hot summer, and by flushing out the backwater swamps they revitalise the waters and provide additional habitats for the summer-breeding cichlid young which have been raised in the shallow backwaters.

The breeding and movements of many fish are adapted to the annual floods. The tide travelling down the main channels is a signal to the tiger fish, which travel upstream to spawn. The exact location of their spawning grounds in the delta is still a mystery, though it might be the secluded reedy 'flats' of the upper delta. After spawning they return to overwinter in the deeper lagoons.

The organic matter and detritus brought down with the floods contributes to the formation of floating swamps or 'peat mats' which play their part in the Delta's constantly changing waterways. As the floodwaters pass through backwater lagoons they slow and deposit their load of detritus in the lagoon; this, together with the mass of decaying vegetation on the bottom of the lagoon, forms a fibrous layer. It is the start of a peat mat, which becomes established as various aquatic plants such as water lilies, bladderworts and water chestnuts begin to give it form and bulk. During the warm summer months the activity of micro-organisms living in the mat produces methane gases which cause the mat to float to the water's surface. Here the aquatic plants can grow and flower. As winter approaches the cold inhibits the activity of the micro-organisms and the mat sinks again. This cycle of wetting and drying eventually stabilises the mat, which no longer sinks and becomes well established with vegetation – in particular with the coarse swamp grass, miscanthus.

The peat mats are useful to many swamp creatures. The swamp worm colonises floating mats; its feeding habits are similar to those of the earthworm, as it consumes vast quantities of organic matter and mud which it then casts onto the surfaces of the mats. The casts are almost pure clay, indicating that swamp worms play an important role in breaking down plant material and making nutrients and oxygen available to other organisms inhabiting the mats. The swamp worm has some interesting adaptations to these low oxygen conditions. It protrudes its hind end above the mud and folds it over to trap a bubble of air, which is pulled back into its burrow. The worm then slowly uses the oxygen in the air bubble, absorbing it through the abundant blood vessels in its 'air chamber'.

Many other creatures rely on the peat mats. Darters perch on them to dry their wings after fishing, and small crocodiles bask on them in the sun. Jacanas frequently land on the mats, where they peck for bloodworms in the lily buds and forage for swamp worms in the mud. In time several peat mats join each other to create larger and larger areas of 'land' which are colonised by miscanthus grass, resulting in extensive regions of peat bog. The miscanthus clumps may grow large enough to block the flow of water in places, and with time they dry out. Permanent beds of grass develop where there used to be water. The final stage to dry land, which may take decades, involves the drying out of the peat mats by smouldering underground fires fed by methane gases. This leaves the bare earth to be colonised by dryland grass. Thus the once-floating peat beds are changed into part of the great floodplain grassland.

The smouldering peat fires of the Delta may also be a result of the blockage of a river channel and its subsequent drying as the waters seek another course. Even major channels in the Okavango are thought to have a life of only a hundred years or so. The death of a watercourse starts when the water is slowed by blockages of vegetation or is lost to other newly-formed drainage systems. The free-floating islands of papyrus and other aquatic plants play an important role; given the fantastic rate at which papyrus grows, it is not long before a small 'plug' of vegetation has grown into a dam some kilometres wide. The traditional river crafts of the local Bushmen and fishermen, the papyrus rafts or wooden dug-outs, may also be a cause of blockage when they are abandoned. The slowing current drops its load of sand, raising the bed of the channel, until finally the water travels elsewhere. The reedbeds on either side of the abandoned channel, which grow on a thick bed of peat, dry out. Here again, methane gases ignite deep within the peat. Many such underground fires smoulder, creating a mosaic of hot patches as lines of smoke rise from the drying reedbeds. The nutrients released by these fires encourage the growth of grasses, and so the reedbeds are converted into more floodplain grasslands. Pools of water may remain, creating an ideal habitat for larger mammals such as buffaloes and lechwes, which now have new pastures interspersed with permanent water. The raised beds of the former channels remain as chains of sandy islands, flanked by the newly formed grasslands.

The drying of river channels, and the change of reedbeds to grasslands, illustrate the dynamic nature of the Okavango's waterways. Small changes may occur in as little as a year; others may happen gradually over many centuries. At the turn of this century there was a major shift in flow from the Thaoge River, which used to flow into Lake Ngami, to the Ngokha and Mborogha systems. This has resulted in the drying of Lake Ngami and the western edge of the Okavango Delta. David Livingstone, the British explorer, was the first European to visit Lake Ngami, reaching it in 1849 after crossing the Kalahari. At that time the lake was some 100 kilometres in circumference. It started shrinking in 1870, due to papyrus blockages upstream; by the early 1900s its former outlet had become its principal inlet. Today Ngami is often dry, a saline lake bed which will eventually resemble the Makgadikgadi Pan if the Thaoge River never flows into it again. In the last twenty years there has been a change in flow between two major rivers, from the Mborogha to the Moanatshira, possibly caused by papyrus blockages. More recently, and on a shorter time scale, the waterways around the south-west of Chief's Island have changed their pattern. These changes result in a mosaic of different habitats which maintains the diversity of the Delta.

The annual flood and the rains are not the only agents of change in Okavango. Surface fires are a common feature in the Delta; three-quarters of the reedbeds are burnt at some time during the year. Papyrus fires are often started by lightning from summer storms, but more commonly fires are started by hunters. The reduction in plant cover makes visibility better, and lechwes and sitatungas are attracted to the flush of new shoots that grow in the reedbeds soon after the fire has passed through. The green papyrus may look unburnable, but its high phenol content (which renders it inedible to many smaller herbivores) makes the plant highly combustible. Once papyrus has caught fire it will burn ferociously. The feathery tops fizzle and burn like firecrackers as, speeded by hot air, the flames race through the reedbeds until they reach the edge of a channel and are extinguished by the water.

During a fire many birds are attracted to the insects disturbed by the flames. Yellow-billed kites and marsh harriers can be seen hovering above, but the bee-eaters are most abundant. From October to December, when the carmine bee-eaters are forming their breeding colonies on the floodplains, a fire attracts large numbers of these beautiful crimson birds. The blue-cheeked bee-eater, a winter migrant from the Middle East, also hunts over papyrus fires. It has an unusual method of catching dragonflies, using a characteristic and spectacular 'back-flip'; the bird glides fast beneath its prey and then momentarily curves its back and head to snap at the insect as it passes overhead. Once the fire is over open-billed storks congregate in large numbers on the charred stubby reedbeds, as it is easier for them to pick off mussels and snails from the exposed papyrus rhizomes.

Elephant activity is yet another feature that can change the pattern of water flow, especially in the phragmites reedbeds. Few creatures can feed on this tall, bamboo-like grass, but elephants love to dig out their roots. Towards the end of the dry season, from September, these largest of land mammals wade out into lagoons to feed on the extensive phragmites reedbeds. Here large herds churn up the reeds and mud as they dig for the tasty roots; soon the elephants are covered in mud and the reedbeds are flattened. They can open up new channels for the water to pass through, while chunks of reeds may float off and block other smaller channels. And the activity of hippos, regularly moving from water to dry land, is another factor in creating and maintaining channels in the reedbeds.

During the floods the area covered by water is doubled in the northern perennial swamps, but increases tenfold as it spills out over the floodplains of the lower Delta. The arrival of the floods in the dry floodplains is a dramatic event. In the southern Delta the scale of the floods is best appreciated from the air and at twilight. The Delta stretches over the horizon; the dark shapes of sand islands and the dusky gold floodplains are surrounded by silver fingers of floodwater shimmering, like threads of mercury, in the sun's dying rays.

The first sign of the flood's arrival in the southern plains is a small trickle of water along a dry watercourse or a well-worn hippo path. Soon the trickle becomes a strong flow, forcing grasses and insects from its path. Migratory fish nose their way along the flooding channels, ready to spawn in the newly enriched habitat. Within a day the narrow channel has over-flowed and shimmering blue water spreads out through the tawny grasses and covers the parched earth.

The effects of the advancing floodwater on plant and animal life are immediate. Ants' nests are submerged, and stranded ants and grasshoppers scramble up the grass stems that remain above water level. They are quickly taken by small fish that travel with the flood-tide. Birds also concentrate on the floodplains to pick up the insects escaping from the flood. Bennett's woodpecker is unusual for a woodpecker, in that it forages mostly on the ground; it is quick to take advantage of the water's arrival, probing with its tongue in the wet mud at the water's edge for stranded ants. The floodwater is enriched as it sweeps over the plains, picking up nutrients from various sources including termite nests, insects, grasses, seeds and animal dung – all things which are not part of the perennially flooded Delta system.

Aquatic creatures are quick to take advantage of the improved feeding conditions. The submerged droppings of floodplain animals are nibbled by tiny cichlid fish. African pike follow the small fish into these shallow flooded areas; they are the main fish predators here, since the water is too shallow for tiger fish. In fact pike and tiger fish, the dominant predatory fish in the Okavango, are closely related species and this separation of habitat helps to prevent competition. Pike need the cover of dense reeds, for they hunt by ambush, watching their prey intently before suddenly striking out. They catch their prey by a sideways swipe, gripping it with razor-sharp teeth and slowly manipulating it before swallowing.

The arrival of the floods in the middle of the cold dry season does not mean that all fish breed at this time. The smaller cichlid fish, in particular, need summer warmth to spawn, regardless of the floods. But more hardy fish, such as the climbing perch and numerous catfish species, take advantage of the rich waters that cover the floodplains to reproduce. The pike also breeds in the watery grasslands and reedbeds soon after the floods arrive. Until recently the spawning behaviour of the African pike was a mystery. It is now known that these fish lay their eggs on a 'nest' of foam. At the onset of breeding, adults form pairs and build foam nests at the water's surface, well hidden in a dense cover of sheltered reeds to protect them from the wind and help the nest keep its shape. Indeed the fish have an extra 'skin flap' on the side of the mouth, which may be used to blow the foam bubbles. The female spawns beneath the nest and numerous large eggs float upwards to become enveloped in the foam nest. The adults then add more foam to the nest, pushing the eggs above water level. Foam nests are a common breeding strategy in swampy habitats, since they keep the eggs from falling onto the sludgy bottom where they would die in the low-oxygen conditions. The foam also prevents the eggs from drying and keeps them in an oxygen-rich environment, and gives a measure of protection against predators.

The pike eggs hatch after a few days. The young fish remain attached to the foam by thin adhesive threads while they live off the remains of the egg yolk sac. After several more days the yolk is exhausted and the small fish become independent and free-swimming. Until this stage the adult pikes have guarded the nest and continued to replenish the foam. When the young fish first leave their nest they are big enough to catch and eat small insects such as mosquito larvae. They grow quickly, developing into fierce little predators that can take prey the same size as themselves – sometimes even their own siblings!

In the mists of a winter's morning, large swarms of mayfly collect over the water's surface and engage in a graceful aerial dance. The members of the swarm are generally all males, since the moment a female enters she is seized by a male and they fly away to mate. The female lays her eggs on the water, where they sink to the bottom and hatch into nymphs. The adult mayflies have small and useless mouthparts and cannot feed, so they die a few days after mating and egg-laying; conversely the nymphs take a year, and sometimes more, to develop. The change from nymph to adult mayfly is one of nature's many wonders. After passing through twenty-three stages, or moults, during its underwater life, the nymph rises to the surface. Here, supported by the surface tension, the nymph's casing splits along its back and the winged 'pro-adult' emerges. Flitting to a reed, the mayfly moults once more into its adult form. This is the only insect in the world known to moult once the wings have become functional.

As the mayflies emerge they are taken by many creatures. If their wings become wet they cannot fly and they are immediately taken by fish. After leaving the water they are taken by birds and bats. Others are caught in the webs of orb-web spiders, which throw gossamer threads between reeds and grasses. The advancing floodwaters bring with them thousands of floating mayflies which have died after their brief adult lives. These accumulate at small blockages and along the edges of the flood, where they are picked out by jacanas and other birds.

The vegetation soon changes as the floodplains are submerged. Delicate pink storm lilies, whose bulbs have remained dormant in the grasslands for a year, burst into flower. Within days snow lilies, sedges and other aquatic plants begin to grow among the submerged grasses, which together with flooded animal dung and drowned insects provide food for fish. In turn the fish in the shallow waters provide easy pickings for numerous fishing birds, which use many different methods to secure their prey. The pied kingfisher hovers for hundreds of wing-beats before it plummets into the water to catch its prey. Enormous saddle-billed storks walk ponderously through the flooded grasses, their eyes focused on the water's surface as they search for a movement they can stab at with their long bills. Their catch is tossed into the air before swallowing. The hammerkop stirs the mud with its feet so as to disturb its favourite prey, the platanna frog, before dexterously spearing it.

For the Delta's larger animals the floods bring a new flush of succulent green vegetation. Lechwes and warthogs wade into the water to graze. So too do waterbucks, though they are much less numerous than their close relatives, the red lechwes. Perhaps they are less well adapted to feeding on the low-quality aquatic vegetation. In front of the flood the earth is softened by the rising water table and here warthogs dig and wallow, covering their skins with cooling mud that keeps away the irritating biting flies. Waterfowl such as the spurwing goose and Egyptian goose, arrive in large flocks and wander along the shoreline, picking at the new green shoots.

The floodwaters cover and restore the grasses that have been so heavily grazed during the dry season. Their arrival pushes many larger animals back to the fringes and interiors of the autumn woodlands, from where they emerge to feed on the remnant grass islands and drink from the fresh water that runs in rivers instead of stagnating in pools. Sable antelopes leave the mopane woods at midday to drink, watching warily for predators. Zebras and giraffes water in the late afternoon, their colours and patterns a perfect foil to the grey bark and russet-gold leaves of the mopane trees that fringe the new water. At dusk herds of elephants emerge from the shade of the woods, scuffing holes on the edges of the flood with their feet to create pools deep enough to drink from. Even the small tree squirrels dare to leave their mopane tree homes to refresh themselves from the new water.

Predators, too, come to the drowning grasslands. The larger carnivores, such as spotted hyaenas, lions and hunting dogs, wade through the shallow water in search of prey. The pack-hunting wild dogs seldom make their kill in water, though spotted hyaenas may run their exhausted and frightened prey into the water, from where there is usually no escape. Vultures spiral over the kills, and the Bateleur eagle soars in lazy circles. Huge herds of zebras and wildebeests, that have roamed the Kalahari interior for most of the year, mass where the Kalahari meets the Delta, as though the scent of the coming flood has drawn them in.

In the shallow floodplains that cover thousands of square kilometres of the lower Delta, after a journey that has taken many months, the last of the Okavango's waters are lost – sucked in by the parched Kalahari sands, burnt off by the sun, and used by innumerable plants and animals. But the river's journey does not quite end here. The lower channels and waterways meet a barrier, the Thamalakane Fault, which marks the southern boundary of the Delta, and eventually they turn abruptly to flow south-east in a single straight channel. Buried beneath 200 metres of sand, the only outward sign of the fault is the river's sudden change in direction. This is the southern boundary of the Delta, the fault which is thought to have caused the ponding back of the Okavango River many thousands of years ago. The river takes the very last of the Delta's water, some two per cent of the flow which arrived in the Panhandle from the Angolan highlands.

This river, the Boteti, carries the Okavango's waters for several hundred kilometres across the Kalahari, in a river valley too wide and deep to be made by such a meagre flow – a reminder of the former size of the Okavango River when it used to flow into Lake Makgadikgadi. Despite the paucity of water, this is a vital river in the Middle Kalahari; indeed, it is the only river. For millennia the wildlife of the region has been able to retreat to the banks of the Boteti when the drought lingered too long. Even now the animals that inhabit the Makgadikgadi Pan and the interior grasslands come here in the dry season. But today the water is in even shorter supply. There is too much competition from cattle, people and the Orapa diamond mine at the end of the river. One hundred years ago Livingstone recorded hunting sitatungas at Lake Xau, an indication of the former lushness of a lake that received the Okavango's waters via the Boteti. Xau now stands dry and desolate, peppered by the skeletons of animals which reached their age-old watering point, found it dry and were too weak to go further. In a very high flood the waters might reach the edges of the Makgadikgadi before they are burnt off in the salt pans amongst the swirling heat and hot springs of this cauldron. More often, however, the last of the Okavango's waters end in a muddy pool, dwarfed by the wide banks of the Boteti and still some kilometres from the ghost of that mysterious lake, Makgadikgadi.

CHAPTER TEN

LAND OF THE HUNTER

Deep in the sandveldt, a small cluster of grass-thatched huts indicates the presence of man. A band of honey-coloured people, lightly clad in skins and beads, set about their daily tasks. Women and children wander into the seemingly barren wilderness with digging sticks and leather bags. Before the day is through they have returned with a feast – delicate truffles dug from the earth; succulent tsama melons; gourdfuls of sun-dried brown berries with the sweetness of raisins; nuts and pods; tasty roots and starchy tubers – the harvest of the Kalahari. The men are out at dawn, after an evening preparing their bows and quivers, spreading poison on their arrowheads and telling stories of past hunts. Lightly and swiftly they step through the sand, looking for tracks, keeping in contact with each other by means of soft, bird-like calls so as not to disclose their presence to the animals they are hunting. From the faint signs in the sand they can tell which species has passed by, what sex and age, at what time and what it was doing. Their quarry is stalked and shot. The poison might take many hours to work, so the wounded creatures must be tracked, then by dusk the meat is taken home. Beneath the Milky Way, which the San call the 'backbone of the sky', there is feasting, dancing and singing all night to celebrate the success of the hunters.

The San, commonly called the Bushmen, are the oldest people of Africa, and the earliest race known to have lived in the Kalahari. Very few remain today, living as their ancestors did. Never in the history of Africa has a people lived for so long on a land without changing or destroying it; their secret is their total dependence on the natural stores of the land. The San live by hunting and foraging, and have never considered it necessary to grow crops or to domesticate animals – they saw no need to, when nature provided them with so much. Their dependence on the land has necessarily taught them to use the wild creatures and wild food wisely – for to over-use and destroy their resources would result in their own destruction.

It is thought that at one time the San occupied most of Africa but gradually, through colonisation by Bantu peoples from the north and south and to a lesser extent the whites from the south, they have lost ground to more ambitious and aggressive races. The Kalahari is the last hunting ground of the San – not because they have been forced there, but rather because this hidden and harsh interior is one of the last areas of Africa to have been settled by other people. The tales the San tell of their origins suggest that once, long ago, they lived in a much lusher and wetter place than today. In the beginning, the story goes, the earth was covered with water; and across the dark waters the Preying Mantis, the legendary hero of the San, was carried by the wise bee. The bee became weary as he searched for dry land, flying lower and lower as the weight of the Mantis dragged him down. Finally he sank to the water, but here the bee suddenly saw a great white flower, perhaps the night lily, half-open in the darkness. The exhausted bee laid the Mantis in the heart of the flower and with it the seed of the first human being, and then he died. But as the first sun's rays warmed the flower, the Mantis awoke; and from the seed left by the bee the first San was born.

Anthropological studies have shown that hunting provides nearly half the San's food requirements. They hunt solely for food – killing for sport is unknown, although hunting is an important social event as well as a way of life. One of the San races are the !Kung people of the western Kalahari. Of the 262 animal species known to them, over eighty are hunted. A few species are taboo. Elephants, for example, are never killed, for the San consider them to have the intelligence of man. Ostriches are seldom killed – they run too fast – but their eggs are prized for food and for ornaments.

Young boys and old men set snares and traps, while the other men hunt the land, shooting larger animals such as antelopes and giraffes with their poisoned arrows. Burrowing species like porcupines, aardvarks and spring-hares are forced out of their burrows, for only the bravest hunter will enter an aardvark burrow to spear this large and powerful creature. In the dry season pits are dug or blinds built near water-holes and salt pans, where the hunters wait to ambush their prey.

The hunting code of the !Kung is based on social values rather than on material gain. A hunter must always remain modest about his kills so as not to create envy amongst others. If he has a series of successful hunts, he will stop hunting for a while to give others a chance to excel. Meat, like everything else, is shared equally amongst the members of a group.

The San's method of making poison for their arrows illustrates just how well they have learnt to use what their environment offers. The toxin is obtained from the pupae of three species of flea-beetle. The two most poisonous species feed on the leaves of the arid-land commiphora bushes, while a third species feeds on marula leaves and is found in wetter localities. The eggs of the flea-beetle are laid in midsummer, around December, and the larvae feed exclusively on the leaves of the bush until they are mature, when they drop to the ground and burrow underground to pupate. Late in the summer the hunters dig deep into the sand around the bushes and collect the pupae. The living pupae are carried in the hunting kit and used as needed. In this form the potency of the poison may last for several months. When needed, a pupa is rolled between the fingers to soften it, and the orange body fluids of the insect spread over the tip of the arrow, or first mixed with acacia gum and saliva to make it extra-adhesive. Once the fluid is out of the pupal cocoon it begins to lose its potency, so arrows have to be touched up if they have not been used.

There is evidence that man lived on the ancient eastern shore-lines of the great Lake Makgadikgadi over 2,000 years ago. On a small mysterious island called Kubu, which juts out into the Makgadikgadi Pans, massive rocks, aligned like fortresses and worn smooth by the pounding of waves long since vanished, now face only the empty burning whiteness of the great salt pans. Only the impassive baobab trees remain. Even today Kubu is sacred to the San people, and it is taboo to collect firewood or in any way disturb the island. Excavations have shown that in addition to hunting zebras, wildebeests and other large animals, the people used fish and aquatic plants for food. Even as the country dried up, these people knew the secret of the land. They never hunted too often in the same place, nor took the tubers, roots and bulbs of the same plants repeatedly. For the San, as for the wild animals of the Kalahari, mobility was the key to survival.

The San were probably the earliest inhabitants of the Okavango Delta. They penetrated the watery wilderness along sand ridges, hunting and foraging for waterlily bulbs and aquatic plants. They made fishing nets from the fibres of wild plants such as aloe and sanserveria, and would also spear or sometimes poison fish in shallow pools by throwing in the dried and ground bark of the motsebe (croton) tree. Their water-craft were rafts of papyrus, on which they drifted downstream or fished from in lagoons. However, their penetration into the depths of the Delta was restricted by the fragile nature of their craft until the arrival of other peoples from the north, who brought with them dug-out canoes.

To the west of the Delta, in the vast sandy expanses of the Kalahari, three granite outcrops rise, massive and brooding, from the flatness. The Tsodilo Hills have attracted people to live around their edges for many thousands of years, perhaps because they are one of the few reliefs in the monotonous sands of the Kalahari. Several thousand paintings on the rock faces tell the tale of the way of life of the peoples that have lived there. Most of the paintings are on west-facing slopes so that they catch the afternoon sun, painted on concave rocks from lofty bluffs that overlook the Kalahari, or on overhangs that act as shelters, or lining stony pathways. Each site seems as carefully chosen as the theme of the painting itself. Wild animals dominate the paintings, expertly executed in ochre colours; each painting still has a meaning to the people that live here. Rhinoceroses were often painted – witchdoctors liked to keep their medicine in hollow rhino horn, and the horn was exchanged with east coast traders for beads and shells. Rhinoceros horns dating from around AD 850 have been found at Tsodilo, suggesting that the climate and variety of animals then were very different from today.

One of the more lively paintings in the hills is of a grotto of naked men dancing with erect penises; the few men without erect penises are the ones in a trance. The scene is believed to depict the Eland Dance, which was performed to cure a person of ailments of the feet. The Gemsbok Dance is performed to cure ailments of the heart, and the Giraffe Dance for ailments of the head. The !Kung people, who still live in the Tsodilo Hills, name illnesses after certain animals, and call on that particular animal to cure the disease.

Some paintings depict a mythical two-horned snake (resembling the head of a giraffe) which controls the water-holes where it lives, determining who can drink and who cannot. The snake is said to bleat like a goat, and rises up with large, shining eyes – in old folk tales the eyes are diamonds, but modern tales represent them as light bulbs! Today a python lives in one of the few springs in the Tsodilo Hills, and the presence of this large, water-loving snake in wet places is no doubt associated with the tale.

The !Kung call the hills 'the bracelets of the morning'. Indeed, after the dark night, the sun's rays bring first one faceted rock face, then another and another to life, the cracked and fissured boulders giving the hills texture and warmth. Filtered sunlight passes between clefts, picking up the earth colours of the rocks – sandstone yellows are washed with warm pinks, and granite grey stone faces are patterned with lime green, white and orange lichens. The sandy paths that weave through the hills pass beneath numerous trees whose leaves catch the morning light as they dance lightly in the breeze. Nearly every bush and tree has a use to foragers, but the most cherished are the mongongo trees, which grow in shady groves in deep Kalahari sands. The mongongo either grows along the ridges of sand dunes, or in pockets of sand near granite outcrops such as Tsodilo. Its occurrence in the deep, waterless sands is as remarkable as the abundance of fruit it produces.

When the fruit first falls its outer flesh is edible, but with time this sweet fruit shrivels and only the nut remains. The almond-flavoured mongongo nut is highly nutritious and is a staple food for the !Kung today, as it has been for many thousands of years. The outer shell is difficult to crack open, and usually the !Kung burn it first. No animals can eat the nuts, although elephants and Kudus feed on the outer flesh. Rainwater collects in the trunks of the older mongongo trees, thus providing the gatherers with water on long foraging trips. Each mongongo grove is individually known to the

!Kung and although they might be in the territory of another clan, the groves and the nuts are freely shared in the spirit of the San people's way of life.

The landscape of Tsodilo has changed little over the centuries; there is no soil erosion, grasses cover the valley floors and fruit-bearing trees such as marulas, mongongos, grewia bushes, acacias and shepherd's trees still grace the rocky valleys and cliffs. They stand as a testament to a way of life that despite millennia of habitation by man has caused so little destruction.

For a long time it was assumed that the San of the Kalahari lived isolated from outside influences until a few centuries ago. But archaeological finds, particularly in the Tsodilo Hills, have shown they have lived in proximity with Bantu pastoralists and traders since at least AD 500. By the third century AD, cattle had become increasingly important, and their remains have been found along with those of wild animals such as zebra, wildebeest, warthog, small game and fish, attesting to the continued importance of hunting despite the presence of domesticated animals. Sea shells indicate there was trade with the Atlantic, while the presence of fish and mussels shows there was local trade with the peoples of the Delta.

The arrival of Bantu peoples from the north, south and west changed the land of the hunter for ever. Their life-style depended on livestock to a greater extent than before. This was perhaps the first time the importance of cattle supserseded that of hunting, for the ownership of cattle came to mean individual wealth, power and freedom from servitude. The rulers controlled the east coast trade in ivory and later gold, and they built up great wealth and power through the ownership of cattle. The BaTswana peoples, Bantu pastoralists from the south, established themselves as the dominant race of people in this region, which was later named Botswana. They brought with them an organised political system, which included a monarchy as well as courts and laws. This hierarchical system put great emphasis on the social status of individuals, which was based on birth-right and wealth through the ownership of cattle. Traditionally the army was of paramount importance, the whole tribe being divided into regiments. Although there was much in-fighting and splitting up of sub-groups, the BaTswana retained their sovereignty over other peoples, and to this day are the rulers of Botswana. For many years they have counted sub-groups with themselves; such a system of incorporation has helped to build a remarkably peaceful nation.

The BaTswana are generally believed to have entered southern Africa between the eleventh and sixteenth centuries in a series of migrations from the north – although it seems likely that earlier BaTswana had already settled south of the Limpopo by the sixth century when they began to replace southern African Stone Age cultures. By the eighteenth century a sub-group of the BaTswana had moved north and settled in what is today Botswana.

The San and BaKgalagadi were already occupying these areas – the Ba-Kgalagadi were a similar ethnic group to the BaTswana, but spoke a different language. The BaKgalagadi and the San were either driven west into the Kalahari, or remained with the BaTswana as their servants. The BaTswana had sheep, cattle and arable crops, which made them rich and powerful in comparison to the hunter/gatherer groups who could not stock-pile the harvest of the land. The BaTswana bought tobacco from eastern tribes and traded this with the BaKgalagadi for wild animal skins, which they made into karosses (skin blankets) and went south to exchange for cattle. The San today are nearly all associated in some way with cattle posts.

Although the BaTswana people traditionally relied on cattle for status and wealth, hunting was such an important source of food that it remained an essential part of society. The central government was built up on a series of regiments, each composed of the young men of a given age group. Apart from looking after a royal boy, their main occupation was to go out hunting, two or three regiments together. After a circumcision ceremony the regiments would also go out and hunt. Status was measured by success or failure in hunting. The hunt was called letsholo. Before the era of guns and motorised transport, there were two main methods of hunting. In the first method pits, known as 'gopos', were dug in the earth at the apex of two fences which funnelled the animals into them. The other method involved teamwork from all the hunters, who stealthily surrounded a group of animals, usually antelopes, closing in on the trapped creatures which were speared as they tried to break through the advancing circle. In the winter they travelled long distances, sometimes journeying a thousand kilometres to the rich hunting grounds of the north. The meat from a season's hunting was dried and brought back to the villages, thus providing an important food supplement. Although this form of hunting died out in the nineteenth century, after the central organisation of the BaTswana broke down, hunting for meat and skins of wild animals continued and to this day is an important supplement for many people, even those that own cattle.

The greatest changes in the peopling of the Middle Kalahari occurred in the last two centuries. Many new groups, refugees from oppressive regimes elsewhere, arrived to make a new home in the relatively untapped and underpopulated Kalahari. The expansion of the Lozi State in north-western Zambia in the 1750s caused two Bantu-speaking groups, the BaYei and the HaMbukushu, to migrate southwards from their homes along the Zambezi River into the Okavango region. Each travelled to different places at different times. It seems that the BaYei were the first to settle in what is now northern Botswana, although it is possible that the Bantu people that lived around the Tsodilo Hills many hundreds of years ago, whose presence is only known through the paintings and archaeological finds, were HaMbukushu. They have a legend that their God, Nyambi, created the first people of their tribe and let them down from heaven on a rope onto the Tsodilo Hills, where the imprints of the first men and their cattle can be seen on the rocks.

The BaYei and HaMbukushu were pastoralists, as well as hunters and fishermen. Since they were moving through areas infested by tsetse fly (the bite of the fly causes a fatal illness in livestock,) they left their stock behind them, and relied instead on hunting and fishing. Coming from the Zambezi River area, they were expert river people and fishermen. They were the first people to introduce the wooden dug-out canoe, called 'mokoros', to the Delta. On these they journeyed through the complex waterways of the north, from the Zambezi and Chobe rivers and down through the Selinda Spillway to join the Okavango Delta system. From there they canoed southwards down the Thaoge River to Lake Ngami, or settled along the many islands and channels where they could live a rich existence, hunting and fishing the quiet unspoilt waters of this enormous system. Such a journey, which included travelling to the former Lake Mababe through the Savuti channel, would now be impossible due to the drying-up of the Selinda and Savuti channels. Their traditional methods of fishing with net baskets are still used today on the inhabited western edges of the Delta.

With the arrival of European traders in search of ivory, ostrich feathers and animal skins in the mid-nineteenth century, a new type of hunter entered the scene. The ivory resources of the country were virtually untouched until this time, and it resulted in the opening up of the 'Lake country' – Lake Ngami, the Okavango Delta and the Kwando and Linyanti swamps. Stories of cattle kraals built of ivory tusks lured commercial hunters who made huge profits from the wildlife resources of the Kalahari. With the arrival of these new traders, with their ox-wagons and guns, great changes occurred – for the inhabitants of the Kalahari were provided with modern firearms. Hunting on a large scale was made possible and this resulted in the indiscriminate and widespread killing of wildlife. As early as 1888, there are records blaming the use of guns for the beginning of the depletion of the wildlife. The BaTswana acted as middlemen between the European traders and the San and BaKgalagadi hunters of the interior. Thus the wealth of the politically powerful BaTswana increased – and the previously flexible social relations between San and Bantu were transformed.

The Herero were one of the last groups of people to settle in the northern Kalahari, bringing with them a way of life more dependent on cattle than that of any other race that lived there. The Herero in Botswana are descendants of refugees who fled South West Africa (Namibia) after an unsuccessful revolution against the German colonialists in 1904. The Herero had entered South West Africa from the lakes of Central Africa around the sixteenth century. There was considerable fighting with the San, the original inhabitants of the area. In 1884 South West Africa was declared a German colony, and the German settlers used the disunity between these two groups to undermine the San, favouring the Herero. By the turn of the century the San had more or less been subjugated, and the Germans turned their attention to the Herero, planning to disarm them, and take their cattle in lieu of debts and taxes. The Herero rose up against the Germans in 1904, but suffered heavy losses. Faced with a campaign of mass killing, the remaining Herero decided to flee through the Kalahari Desert, to join relatives who had settled in northern Botswana some ten years earlier. During their flight they lost all their cattle, and started their new life as servants to the few established Herero with cattle, or to the BaTswana who were the political leaders of the country. In return for labour they received milk and cattle. They slowly built up their herds, using their considerable expertise in cattle management. In this way most had reached economic independence within twenty years. Today they have an unmistakable air of self-confidence and pride.

Although there were no boreholes in the Kalahari until this century, permanent villages became established at various pans which then had permanent water. During the rains the stock moved deep into the sandveldt, following the good grazing and only returning to the permanent cattle posts when the Kalahari dried. For the first time an animal was introduced that competed for the Kalahari's precious resources of grass and water. Since these pastoralists preferred to save their cattle, which were their wealth and a form of currency, hunting continued to be important. Furthermore, in times of drought, or when people were forced to move because of war, wild animals once again became the resource of the country on which people depended. Wild plants, wildlife and fish continued to be as important to the later inhabitants of the Kalahari and the Delta as they had been to its ancient hunter/gatherer inhabitants.

But the teeming wildlife of the Kalahari was not an inexhaustible resource. The start of commercial hunting with modern weapons, and the expansion of cattle into the grasslands of the Kalahari, gradually reduced those vast herds of wild animals, which for thousands of years had provided man with food and clothing. But it is only in the last thirty years, with the rapid and large-scale expansion of Botswana's cattle industry, that the Kalahari's wildlife and the grasses on which it depends – a resource that was free to the people and was expected to last for ever – has been seriously threatened. For the first time it has become necessary to restrict and control hunting, and to protect areas of land from the advancement of cattle.

The great expansion of Botswana's cattle industry began in the 1950s, when modern technology made it possible to drill deep boreholes which tapped ancient waters trapped deep in the earth. For the first time man and his domesticated beasts occupied the waterless regions of the Kalahari

To the west of the Delta's Panhandle, three granite outcrops rise from the flat Kalahari sands. The Tsodilo Hills (bottom), called 'the bracelets of morning' by the !Kung San, have been inhabited by man for several thousand years.

Most of the rock paintings found on the rock faces of Tsodilo (below) depict wild animals, and attest to the continued importance of hunting to the people who lived there. Nature's art is in evidence on rock faces covered by colourful lichens (bottom).

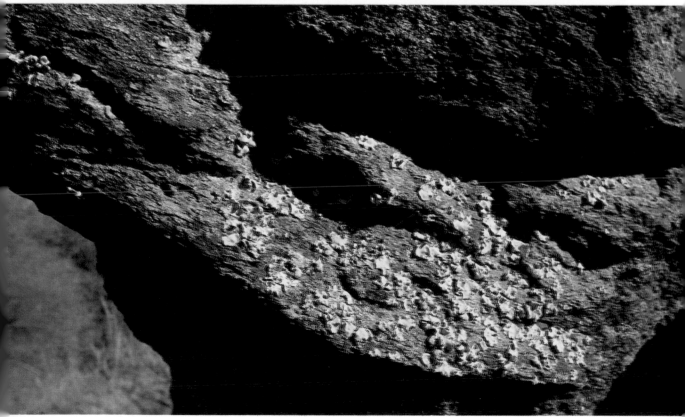

The traditional San dress of skins and beads is being replaced by western-style clothing, but the San woman (below) still wears her colourful beads, while the old hunter and his son (opposite bottom) illustrate the merging of old ways and new. In the Delta some BaYei women still fish using their traditional baskets (opposite top).

Baskets are woven from the young leaves of *Hyphaene* palms (opposite). The fine quality of this traditional craft is making Botswana baskets a thriving industry. Herero women walk through their cattle post (below) – their petticoats and bonnets are perhaps a legacy from the German occupation of their former home, Namibia.

Too many animals in one place for too long results in overgrazing (opposite). Increasingly, wild animals are dying of starvation as a result of competition with cattle for food. Fences were built to control the spread of foot-and-mouth disease in cattle: the Buffalo Fence around the Delta (below) and the Makalamabedi Fence beyond the Boteti River (bottom).

The need for cattle to drink daily (below) creates problems as cattle posts penetrate the Kalahari – formerly the domain of mobile and light-footed animals. The draining of floodplains (opposite) to extract water from the Delta will affect subsistence farmers dependent on the annual floods to grow crops.

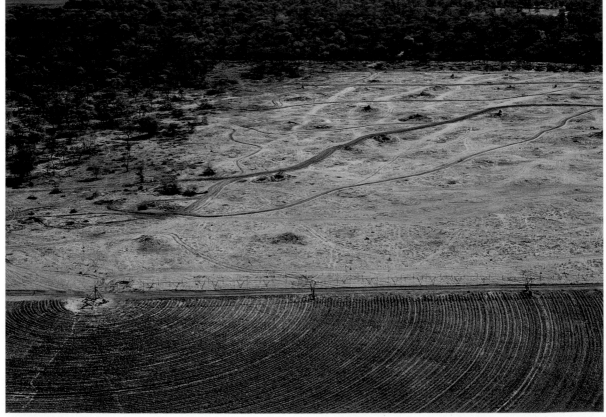

Large areas of the Delta are sprayed (below) to control tsetse flies, which transmit a deadly parasite – but no one knows what effect chemical 'cocktails' have on wildlife. Fires, often started by man, burn over 70% of the Delta each year (opposite top). Irrigated farming will help Botswana increase its food production (opposite bottom).

222 Salvinia (inset) is an exotic weed which quickly infests African waters, choking aquatic life and blocking waterways. An outbreak in the Lower Delta in 1986, presumably brought in from the Kwando and Linyanti swamps, covered Xini Lagoon within weeks (below).

Hippos (below) also contribute to the dispersal of the salvinia weed, and so a fence was built around Xini Lagoon to restrict their movement further into the Delta. The outbreak was controlled by pumping the lagoon dry, but the possibility of another outbreak in the Delta will always be of concern.

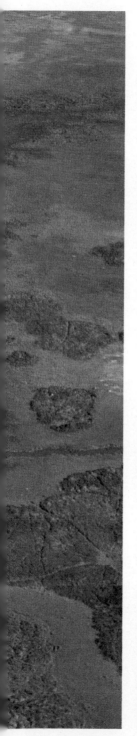

Opposite: The Orapa diamond mine (top) is one of three in Botswana, providing the country with its most important source of revenue.
Tourism will need to be controlled in order to protect the wilderness that visitors come to experience (bottom).

225

sandveldt and were able to utilise the vast unspoilt grasslands. During the high rainfall periods of the 1950s, the abundant growth of grass in the rejuvenated Kalahari encouraged great increases in the number of cattle. Traditionally African pastoralists were able to move to new areas when the grasslands became overgrazed; mobility meant they did not have to limit the size of their herds. However, in the Kalahari the need for cattle to drink daily restricts them to grasslands within a day's walk from the boreholes; and their numbers must be controlled if the grasslands are to survive.

For thousands of years, the Kalahari was inhabited only by wild animals that had evolved to survive in this fragile, arid land. The grazing animals are delicately built, light of foot and highly mobile. All but the wildebeest are independent of drinking water. Heavy-hooved and massive, cattle must trudge to the same watering point daily, and are thus restricted to a small range. Small wonder the heavily grazed grasses died out to scrub, and the trudging hooves, repeatedly following the same path to water, kicked out shallow-rooted plants, allowing the wind to carry away the freed sand. A widening circle of naked sand began to spread around each borehole, and the patchwork of overgrazed range slowly extended as more and more boreholes were sunk, and more people and cattle settled.

The spread of cattle into these regions of the Kalahari was to have a far-reaching and dramatic effect on the wild animals – both directly, through competition for grasses and loss of their former range, and indirectly through the building of fences which interrupted the movement of wild animals. These fences included border fences, separating Botswana from neighbouring Namibia and South Africa, fences along major roads, and a vast network of veterinary cordon fences built to control cattle movement. The first of the country's veterinary cordon fences were being strung out across the land at about the same time as the first deep boreholes were being sunk. These fences were designed to control the spread of foot-and-mouth disease. This highly contagious disease occurs in both buffalo and in resistant African cattle without causing them any harm, but it is feared by the farmers of Europe where the disease can spread like wildfire, and infected meat must be destroyed. Foot-and-mouth disease can ruin farmers. In 1958 there was an outbreak in Botswana, and no meat could be exported. The northern Buffalo Fence was built to prevent contact between wild buffalo (potential carriers of the disease) and domestic cattle, while the other fences act as buffer quarantine zones, built to comply with the strict import regulations of the EEC, which now takes 50 per cent of Botswana's beef.

Over 3,000 kilometres of fences now carve up much of Botswana. The fences, particularly those built in the 1950s and early 1960s, were erected with little knowledge or forethought of their impact on the habitat and its wild animals. The Kuke Fence stretches for 300 kilometres across the Kala-

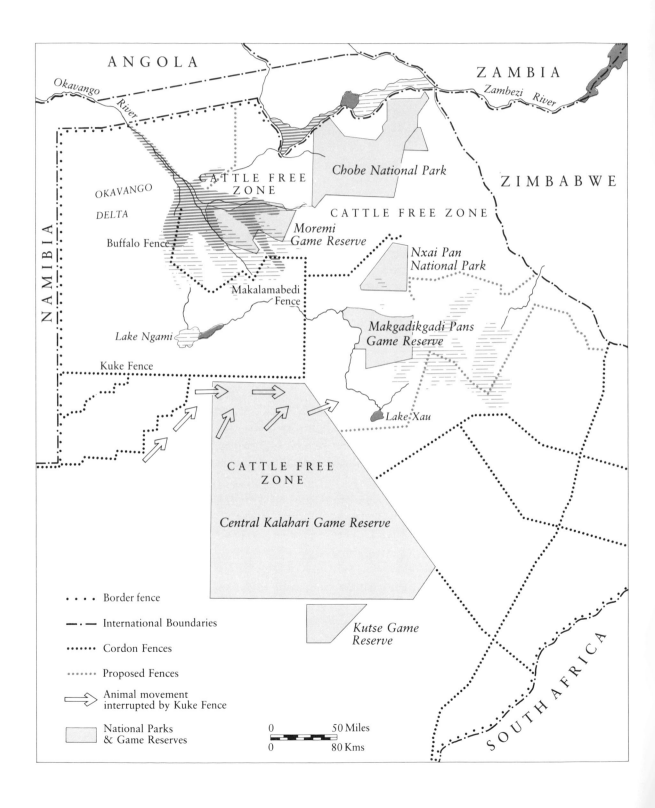

ANGOLA

ZAMBIA

Okavango

River

Zambezi River

ZIMBABWE

NAMIBIA

OKAVANGO

DELTA

CATTLE FREE
ZONE

Chobe National Park

CATTLE FREE ZONE

Buffalo Fence

Moremi
Game Reserve

Nxai Pan
National Park

Makalamabedi
Fence

Makgadikgadi Pans
Game Reserve

Lake Ngami

Kuke Fence

Lake Xau

CATTLE FREE
ZONE

Central Kalahari Game Reserve

Kutse Game
Reserve

SOUTH AFRICA

· · · · Border fence

— · — International Boundaries

· · · · Cordon Fences

· · · · · · Proposed Fences

⇨ Animal movement
interrupted by Kuke Fence

☐ National Parks
& Game Reserves

0   50 Miles

0   80 Kms

hari, almost dividing Botswana in half and separating the large animals of the waterless sandveldt of the central Kalahari from the great water crescent of the north – the Okavango Delta, the Kwando and Linyanti swamps and the Chobe River. In the past, these well-watered areas were always available to animals in times of drought, enabling a large proportion of the water-dependent animals to survive. These were then able to return to the Kalahari interior when conditions improved.

It is in times of drought, when the rains fail for several consecutive years, that the frailty of the land is revealed. And so the drought of the early 1960s showed the devastation that man and his stock could bring to the grasslands. The build-up of cattle around their fixed life-line of water rapidly depleted the grazing, and thus the food supply of all grazing animals. The fences blocked the paths of migratory animals to their dry-season sources of water. The species most seriously affected was the wildebeest, since they are totally dependent on grass for food and, unlike the true Kalahari residents, they need to drink water when the grasses dry out. For them cattle are serious competitors. In 1963, some 300,000 wildebeest died of starvation around Nata. With the drought huge herds, numbering over a million animals, scattered in lines across the vast Kalahari, heading northwards to fresh grass and water as they had done in the past. After trekking for days, even weeks, the movement of thousands of hungry and thirsty wildebeests was halted by the seemingly innocuous strands of wire of the Kuke Fence. Unable to travel northwards they turned east, travelling along the lines of the fence. Many died along the fence, but thousands were channelled to the end of the fenceline where there was once a source of water – Lake Xau, the end point of the Boteti River and the last drop of the Okavango's water. However, this is an area of communal grazing, settled by people and heavily grazed by their cattle. The bewildered wildebeests, concentrated unnaturally by the fences, died of starvation on finally reaching the water. So unexpected was this tragic interference with the forces of nature that it is not fully known just how many wild animals died.

In the next decade better rains replenished the grasses and the Kalahari once more came to life. Like a bad dream, the horrors of the 1960s' drought were forgotten. The wild animals no longer had to migrate, for there was food and water for them in the Kalahari interior and the herds recovered. With good grazing and more water the cattle herds, too, increased. There was a new incentive to cattle owners: the EEC had formed an aid and trade agreement giving Botswana a substantial rebate on the import levy. This rebate is paid at the end of each year and is then divided amongst the cattle owners according to the amount of meat they sold. In this way the growers of foot-and-mouth-free beef received sixty per cent more than the true world market value of beef. This agreement, known as Lome 3, is valid until 1990 when it will be renegotiated. The national herd increased from 1 million to 3.5 million head in just over a decade.

With the drought years of the 1980s the cycle once more repeated itself, but on a larger scale than ever before. Even the casual observer could see that in drought conditions, which are so frequent as to be the norm, over-grazing was destroying large areas of Botswana's valuable grasslands. The situation is most severe in the communal grazing lands, where grazing is free. Seventy per cent of the national herd grazes here, including animals belonging to private ranches. With no particular individual responsible for the management of the area, overstocking is severe and the grasslands are seriously damaged. Most areas simply cannot support the numbers of cattle grazing on them. Two independent surveys, carried out in 1980 and 1985, estimated the optimal stocking rate of the central Kalahari grasslands as approximately one livestock 'unit' per sixteen hectares; they currently carry twice this density. Overgrazing is probably the most serious environmental problem facing Botswana today, as it enters its sixth consecutive year of drought.

With the drought the fences once more took their toll. Thousands of hartebeests died along fences to the west of the country. The wildebeests once more migrated northwards, and were again channelled to Lake Xau where they faced severe competition with cattle for grass and water. In 1983 52,000 of the 80,000 wildebeests at Lake Xau died. In 1985 only 11,000 wildebeests arrived at Lake Xau, 2,000 of which died. In 1986 there was no migration, and the lake was dry. Although wildebeests have great resilience and the ability to increase rapidly after bad years, there is a limit to the losses a population can sustain. The population has already crashed. Aerial surveys in 1987 counted only 260 wildebeests in the central Kalahari. Zebras, buffaloes and elephants became extinct there earlier this century; wildebeests are likely to follow.

The fences cannot be entirely blamed for the tremendous loss of wildlife in the western, central and southern parts of the country. Cattle are com-peting for land; many animals died of starvation and not just thirst. The long periods of drought have killed large numbers of cattle as well as wild animals. Even if the Kuke Fence were removed today, the wildlife of the central Kalahari would meet with a barrier of cattle posts, people and overgrazed range before reaching the Okavango Delta. Ironically the Kuke Fence now prevents cattle from entering the Central Kalahari Game Reserve. Furthermore not all fences have been catastrophic to wild animals. The Buffalo Fence, around the south-eastern edge of the Okavango Delta, was built to keep buffaloes (potential carriers of foot-and-mouth disease) from cattle. Since the fence confines wild animals to a well-watered area it does not interrupt any outward migration and it serves as a useful barrier between the wilderness of the Delta and the increasing number of people and cattle at its edges. The tragic loss of wildlife along the Kalahari's fences does, however, stand as a testament to the fragile nature of the Kalahari and to the need for forethought and planning before making other changes to the land. In 1987 another veterinary cordon fence was planned, which was to stretch along the north of the Makgadikgadi Pans to the border with Zimbabwe. The conservation body of Botswana, the Kalahari Conservation Society, pointed out to the government the damage such a fence would have on wildlife, and its course has now been realigned to minimise its interference with migratory movements.

Pressure from people, cattle and fences, exacerbated by the long drought, has had a damaging effect on many wildlife populations. Herds of migratory animals such as wildebeests, hartebeests and elands have been reduced to a fraction of their former size. The numbers of giraffes, gemsboks and kudus decreased during the drought. The reduction in the numbers of so many herbivores has also disrupted predator populations. And so the land of the hunter has suffered. Until the 1980s over sixty per cent of the people of western Botswana depended on hunting to supplement their livelihood. Now many people must travel further and further from their settlements, perhaps a journey of two or three days, to find animals to hunt. Whereas before people relied on wildlife for food, they now depend increasingly on drought relief aid.

To the north of the Kuke Fence the range is virtually free except for the Makalamabedi and the Buffalo Fences. Animals can move freely over a vast area which comprises the Makgadikgadi Pans, the northern woodlands, and the great northern water crescent. The watery wilderness of the Okavango covers some 18,000 square kilometres and is virtually uninhabited by man and his livestock. This northern region of Botswana forms one of the last great wilderness areas remaining in Africa today. The great variety of habitats is matched by a breathtaking variety and abundance of wildlife. It is unique in that the arid-land animals of the Kalahari, such as gemsboks and brown hyaenas, are found almost side by side with specialists of swamps and rivers, such as sitatunga and hippopotamuses. Migrations of wildebeests and zebras still occur on a large scale in this area, unhindered by fences. Recent surveys by the Wildlife Department in these northern regions have counted a population of 50,000 elephants, one of the largest savanna elephant populations in Africa. The Wildlife Department has radio-collared a large sample of elephants; results show that they roam widely, even crossing into Zimbabwe. In the dry season they concentrate along the rivers and swamps, but with the first rains they are still able to wander deep into the wilderness of the interior, covering several hundred kilometres on their journey. The survival of this northern wilderness and its fauna depends on wild animals being able to wander freely in search of food and water and on the protection of the fragile grasses and wetlands from cattle.

Botswana has a valuable wildlife resource which has long been recognised by the government. In 1956, at the time that the cattle industry began expanding and the first veterinary cordon fences were being erected, a government department was formed to administer wildlife conservation. The department's work was backed up by modern conservation policies when the Fauna Conservation Act, a legislation with great powers, was drawn up in 1963. With the awareness that the wild animals of their land were a diminishing resource, the government began to set aside large areas as sanctuaries. Seventeen per cent of the total land area is set aside as national parks and reserves, and Botswana remains one of the few countries in Africa where large numbers of wild animals occur outside the parks and reserves. Since these protected areas are not ecologically complete units, their size and shape being determined more by the need to avoid people and settlements, it is important to wildlife that the outlying areas remain free so that animals can follow their traditional pattern of movements.

The decline of wildlife has worried the people of northern Botswana as well as the government. As traditional hunters they were concerned about the loss of wildlife, and the possibility of animals disappearing for ever, for many relied on hunting for food, and considered wild animals an inexhaustible resource which would be passed on to their children and their children's children. Thus the BaTswana people living on the eastern edge of the Okavango Delta agreed to the formation of a wildlife reserve on their land, where animals could live and reproduce in peace without harassment from hunters – the local hunters as well as the big professional hunting companies which had arrived in Botswana from East Africa in search of new hunting grounds. This bold step, which meant many people had to move, created Moremi Wildlife Reserve – the first wildlife sanctuary in southern Africa created by an African tribe on their own land. It is the only protected area within the Okavango Delta, and is of great importance to Botswana.

Hunting is still of tremendous importance in Botswana. Free-roaming wildlife is now declared a national resource, held in trust by the state for the people and future generations. Although people could once hunt freely, hunting laws have had to be introduced because of the increasing pressure on wild animals. These laws are complex since they must recognise the traditional rights of the various groups who live on state land, tribal land, or depend on wildlife for their food like the San Bushmen. To match these there are different categories of hunting licences: special licences for subsistence hunters (these are free, but traditional hunting methods must be used); licences for citizens of Botswana, which cost very little; and licences for non-resident foreigners which cost considerably more. Hunting fees bring considerable revenues to the government, and could bring in even more. They are the least expensive licence fees in Africa, even those for visitors. Although a licence to hunt zebras costs about £37 sterling, a zebra skin can be sold for more than four times that amount to taxidermists.

Every hunter in Botswana must take out a licence. Hunting licences specify which animals can be shot and how many. There are quotas for different species, and the hunting of certain species, such as elephants and brown hyaenas, is prohibited. Licences must be filled in and returned. Bird hunting has very high kill limits, and hunters do not have to fill in a return, so there is the potential for abuse. The recent computerisation of the hunting licence system has yielded valuable information and will help to control licence offences. It has now been shown that a large number of the animals being shot are not recorded, since many people do not send in their returns. The computerisation, the first system of its kind in Africa, will help detect offences, and provide a rapid means of evaluating hunting quotas.

Much of Botswana is divided into controlled hunting areas. Most are open to all hunters, with the proviso that no more than six hunters operate in any controlled hunting area in a week. Fifteen hunting areas are leased to the large professional hunting safari companies on an annual basis. Money from these concessions goes directly to the local Land Board which is responsible for administering the area. These concessions are not heavily utilised, and there is a six-month closed season from November to April, so they remain as wilderness areas. Professional hunting has become an important industry in Botswana – as well as providing employment and meat, there are large profits to be made in the sale of skins, and further employment in the preparation and export of trophies. Professional hunting provides a high rate of financial return per animal shot. In 1985 big-game hunting earned £1.5 million in foreign exchange even though only five per cent of the permitted quota of animals was shot. This means each animal killed by professional hunters earned Botswana £731 sterling.

The beauty of the Okavango and the spectacular wildlife heritage of Botswana attracts a large number of visitors, who come to view animals, or to enjoy the tranquillity of the wilderness. Tourism has become an important industry, the fourth-largest income earner after diamonds, cattle and copper-nickel. Over one thousand jobs are created directly through tourism – the greatest employer of people of any economic sector in northern Botswana. However, like any other development in the Delta, tourism will need to be controlled so as not to damage the very wilderness that people come to experience.

Realising the potential value of wildlife, the government has developed the Wildlife Conservation Policy. In addition to hunting and tourism, wildlife farming could also be an important source of revenue. Wild animals can be 'farmed' to provide meat, skins and trophies. Crocodile farms and ostrich farms have already been established. There are plans to create more wildlife ranches in marginal areas, where the water-independent species of the Kalahari are better able to survive than cattle. By raising different species of wild animals, which feed on different types of vegetation, a given area of land can produce three times as much protein as cattle on the same range. There are also proposals to convert large areas of land into 'wildlife management areas', where the commercial exploitation of wildlife, in all its various forms, can take place. These will act as buffer zones between the national parks and reserves and areas settled by people and livestock.

Momentum is gathering in an effort to conserve Botswana's valuable wildlife heritage, as well as to provide an economic return. In 1987, the EEC gave the Botswana government a grant of 1.1 million pula (£450,000 sterling) to wildlife. The money is partly being spent on undertaking a country-wide aerial survey to count the number of wild animals and determine their distribution. The results are analysed on computers and the results immediately used by the Wildlife Department to make policy decisions. A low count of hartebeests in the west of the country resulted in their immediate protection from hunting. Money will also be spent on expanding the Wildlife Training Centre, which recruits and trains people for posts in the Wildlife Department.

The Botswana government has initiated the National Land Management and Livestock Project, funded by a loan from the World Bank. The project aims to address the problem of overgrazing and bad livestock management in communal grazing areas. New abattoirs will be built to encourage a higher turn-over of cattle, and better education in ranch management will be provided. The objectives are to improve the quality of existing cattle areas, rather than to extend them. A significant effort is being made to formulate land-use plans throughout the country for, as the economy expands, there is growing conflict over the way given areas of land should be used. In the north this will include the separate zoning of tourist areas and hunting areas; the control of tourist activities in the Okavango Delta; selecting areas of ecological importance which should be left undisturbed; and the establishment of wildlife management areas and game ranches.

There are fears that the cattle industry will continue to expand northwards, and that the pattern of overgrazing and loss of wildlife will be repeated. The growing commitment of the government to conservation makes one optimistic that this will not occur. But to remain as a national asset wildlife must be able to hold its own against cattle. Does wildlife pay? Can wildlife compete with cattle economically? The cattle industry receives in the order of thirty times the investment that the wildlife industry receives. Despite this, wildlife has shown an economic return in the order of seventeen times the expenditure by the government and, with the proposed improvements in wildlife utilisation, the returns could be much greater.

The future protection and utilisation of wildlife will also depend on the incentives provided to individuals. Cattle have always been of traditional importance for status and wealth. Wildlife must be shown to benefit individuals more directly if it is to be considered as an alternative to cattle. This could take the form of money paid to tribal land boards and councils for use of the land (as happens already with hunting concessions), and for licences sold – essentially some share of the profits.

Can wildlife compete with cattle? Time will tell, but despite the fact that the world's wilderness and wild animals are becoming increasingly scarce, the answer could well be yes.

CHAPTER ELEVEN

DIAMOND DELTA

The last of the Okavango's waters flow along the Boteti River. Snaking across the Kalahari, they flow towards the edges of the Makgadikgadi Pans. Here, deep beneath the sands, not far from the Okavango Delta, is Orapa, the second biggest diamond pipe in the world. For some ninety million years, it lay hidden in the vast flatness of the Kalahari's sandveldt, unmarked by any striking features or change in topography.

Diamonds, the hardest substance known on earth, are formed of pure carbon, crystallised from the heat and stress of ancient volcanoes, hidden deep within the earth in volcanic pipes. Few of nature's resources occur as rarely as a diamond pipe; yet of only seven major diamond pipes to have been found in Africa, three occur in Botswana. Today diamonds are Botswana's greatest industry. The story of how diamonds were found there is as romantic as the aura attached to the elusive stone itself.

The search for diamonds in the huge and then largely uncharted territory of Botswana was initiated in 1955 by De Beers, the giant company that sells most of the world's diamonds. A team of geologists, led by Gavin Lamont, began their long search in the dry beds of sand rivers that leave the Kalahari to the south. For a long time they found nothing at all. Then, temptingly, three small diamonds were discovered in the dry seasonal river bed of the Motloutse, a tributary of the Limpopo. The team endlessly searched the river, travelling up the gentle slope towards its headwaters, seeking the pipe from which the diamonds had come. Their methodical prospecting revealed nothing.

The team did not give up. Lamont's attention was caught by the theory of another great geologist, Alex Du Toit – the man who first proposed the theory of continental drift and the breaking up of Gondwanaland. He suggested that those tectonic rumblings that broke apart continents also caused the land to buckle and warp, and that this created valleys, built rifts and diverted the course of rivers. It was possible that the upper Motloutse had been separated from its lower course by a warp in the earth's crust, and that the true headwaters of the river lay on the opposite side of the slope they were prospecting. So the geologists continued their search in the vast Kalahari sand face to the north. Finally, twelve years after the search for diamonds began in Botswana, some tell-tale garnets, brought up by the activity of termites which sometimes tunnel hundreds of metres into the earth for water, were found in the wilderness near the Makgadikgadi Pans. Within weeks a massive diamond pipe was discovered, deep within the sands. It was called Orapa, after a lonely cattle post nearby. The find confirmed the existence of the Kalahari–Zimbabwe Fault, which had cut off the headwaters of the river at the point where diamonds were first discovered. It was this very fault that had caused the ponding back of the Kalahari's northern rivers and created the ancient Lake Makgadikgadi, on the edges of which the diamond pipe was found.

Diamonds require great quantities of water to be extracted from the earth. It is perhaps a bitter irony that such a massive diamond pipe should be located in the arid Kalahari, on the shores of an ancient lake long since dry. Although Orapa lies within 280 kilometres of the Delta, only a small fraction of the Okavango's vast resources of water reach it via the Boteti River. In the 1970s a large reservoir was developed from a natural pan to store the Boteti's floodwaters after their long journey from the Angolan highlands through the Okavango Delta. The flow of one of the Okavango's rivers, the Boro, was increased by dredging a stretch of its river bed and blocking some of its outlets with earthen dams. For several years the Mopipi reservoir was full, but the drought years of the 1980s reduced the floods to such an extent that the waters of the Boteti never reached Mopipi reservoir and Lake Xau beyond. The diamond mine has once more resorted to boreholes, which drill deep into the earth for trapped fossil waters. These groundwaters are very ancient, and it is thought they will dry up long before the productive life of the mine comes to an end in roughly one hundred years.

Extensive explorations of the groundwater reserves in the region are under way, and the results are needed before a decision can be made on whether Orapa will need additional surface water. It seems likely that Orapa will have to look elsewhere for its waters; and surveys are currently under way to find a sensible way of utilising the waters of the Okavango Delta.

There are, however, widespread fears that the extraction of water from the Okavango Delta will upset the delicate natural balance of a complex system, still little understood by man. In the past there have been many attempts to influence the flow of the Delta's water, and in hindsight most of them have been remarkably misguided. Hydrologists, government officials, hunters, explorers and researchers have all attempted at some time to cut their way through channels blocked by papyrus, or to open up new channels as they tried to tame the swamps. Small earthen dams (called 'bunds') have been built to improve the water supply to areas of flood irrigation. In the 1970s, large areas of floodplain were drained when the Boro River was dredged to improve the flow of water down the Boteti River to Orapa. The unflooded land reverted quickly to its arid origins.

Other grandiose schemes for using the Okavango's waters have included a proposal for an aqueduct to take water from the Delta to Pretoria in South Africa. Another suggested a 1,000-kilometre canal, large enough to be navigable, from the Panhandle to the capital city, Gaborone, in the south; the route would be across the Kalahari sand face. A particularly wild proposal was that the Okavango and Chobe rivers be diverted into the Makgadikgadi Pans, thus creating a huge lake. The idea was that the lake would increase evaporation, thus resulting in heavier rainfall, which in turn would increase the flow of the rivers. In this way vast quantities of water would be available for irrigation, changing the Kalahari into 'the most fertile region in the world'. As one economist noted, these ideas 'were based on complete ignorance of topographic levels, very unsound meteorological theory and at times very dubious arithmetic'! Fortunately for the Okavango, and for future generations of Botswanan people, these ideas remained untested dreams. The Okavango's waters remain untampered by the wild schemes of man.

The Okavango Delta is of particular value in the Kalahari, since it comprises one of the few sources of water in a vast inland plateau of aridity. The Okavango Delta is a major water resource of Botswana, and its water will be increasingly in demand for the nation's development, for its people, for agriculture and livestock, and for exploiting its great mineral wealth. The Botswana government has financed a large-scale survey of the land and water potential around the southern edges of the Delta. They are examining ways of taking the Delta's water for irrigated farming, as well as to supply Maun township, and ultimately Orapa, with water. The government is anxious for Botswana to become self-sufficient in food production, and looks to the Okavango for water to irrigate crops.

Unfortunately, very few of the soils around the southern Delta are suitable for intensive farming. Some are very acidic, while others are highly alkaline. Moreover, the soils are generally infertile, have poor moisture retention, and are easily blown away by the wind. One of the problems with irrigation is that the resulting evaporation brings salts to the surface which poison the soil; farming techniques to overcome this, such as hydroponics, are very expensive and need a high level of management. Compounding these problems is the great distance to markets due to the remoteness of the Okavango – some 500 kilometres from the nearest railhead. The produce from large-scale, intensive irrigation would probably have to be subsidised.

A traditional method of flood irrigation, called molapo farming, occurs around the fringes of the Delta, particularly in the west, and depends on the natural flooding of the Delta to irrigate the crops. This method of farming has many advantages over more intensive methods: it is labour intensive and thus creates work; the soils are rested for part of the year; when the floods arrive they flush away any accumulated salts; and the floods bring with them plant and animal material which acts as a natural fertiliser. This system of irrigation is inexpensive, and at the same time a balanced way of using the natural flood regime of the Delta. The Southern Okavango Development Water Project is now committed to improving areas of molapo farming, rather than to intensively irrigating large areas of unsuitable land. The demand for water is therefore less than originally anticipated.

The findings and recommendations of the project are currently being reviewed by the government. Whether intensive irrigation is feasible at present is open to debate, but water is still needed for Maun, the gateway of the north, as well as for Orapa diamond mine. Both depend on rivers that carry away the last of the Okavango's waters, but as the drought continues there are worries that when the floods are too low there is not enough water to meet increasing demands. The project is divided into several phases, the first of which is to build a reservoir to supply water to Maun. It is likely that this first phase will be carried out, since its economic benefits are high, and the land to be flooded has already been damaged by overgrazing.

However, the other phases of the project are causing concern over their effect on the fragile natural balance of the Delta. The second phase of the project aims to increase the flow of one of the rivers draining the Okavango, the Boro River. This would be done by dredging the river for some thirty-six kilometres to deepen and widen it, thus cutting through the Kunyere Fault-line, which ponds back the lower Delta's water, and penetrating deep into the Delta. Small tributaries of the Boro would be blocked by a series of earthen dams.

The extraction of water from the lower Delta will inevitably drain large areas of seasonal swamps. This would reduce the amount of land flooded and would therefore seriously affect the way the whole system is revitalised each year by the coming of the nutrient-rich floodwaters. The environmental impact study associated with the project has estimated that seventy square kilometres of floodplain will be drained, including the feeding grounds of water birds, notably endangered species such as wattled cranes and slaty egrets. The breeding and movement of fish in the Delta are also closely adapted to the annual floods. The floods enrich the lower waters and create vast shallow inundated areas which are used by fish for feeding and breeding. The floods also provide a means of distributing fish through the Delta. The dredging of the Boro will inevitably disrupt the fish population, and the breeding grounds of those fish that populate the more southerly waters of the Thalamakane and the Boteti.

People will also be affected, particularly those inhabiting the areas that will be drained. Hunters will lose animals, molapo farmers their waters, and all inhabitants will lose access to wild foods and reeds and leaves for building and weaving. Roads will open up previously inaccessible areas of the Delta to heavy works machinery for construction work and maintenance. The Boro River is important to tourism, giving people access into the Delta from Maun, and is used for boat trips and fishing. Channelling the river will destroy the beauty and wildness that attract so many people to the area.

Water extraction schemes must take into account the fact that the average life of a river before it changes course may be as little as one hundred years; this means that, because of the changeable nature of the Delta's water flow, many proposals are simply not practical. Lake Ngami is an example of this. Ever since the first outsiders reached Lake Ngami 150 years ago, there have been ideas on how to use it. Even 100 years ago it was suggested that a town be built on the lake's shores, and large areas of land irrigated. The lake dried up after the Thaoge River changed course. If any one river channel in the lower Delta is dredged to extract water there is a possibility that in the future its course will change and that the channel will, over time, continue to be extended in order to capture more water. Once money has been sunk into a project, there will be the temptation to continue rather than to abandon and seek an alternative. The end result could be a series of canals criss-crossing the Delta, penetrating into its very heart as they chase the changeable waters.

The Department of Water Affairs has committed itself, however, to not interfering with the perennial swamps. Following the findings of the environmental impact team, it has been agreed to abandon alternative water extraction projects deep in the Delta. It is also possible that the dredging of the Boro will not take place, particularly since the unsuitability of soils means that large quantities of water are not immediately needed for irrigation. The final outcome may depend on the urgency with which Orapa needs water.

There are alternatives, although they will take longer to reach fruition and will be more expensive. One option is to extract water by pipeline from the Panhandle, where the Okavango flows as a swift river. The effect of taking a small percentage of water there would be diluted as the waters spread over the vastness of the Delta, having a minimal effect on the lower floodplains in any single area. A study by the United Nations Food and Agriculture Organisation in 1976 recommended that as much as ten per cent of the Okavango's waters could be taken off at the Panhandle without appreciably affecting the outflow.

A canal is already under construction, excavating a disused channel and by-passing a thick papyrus blockage on the Thaoge River. This will supply water to molapo farms along the western edges of the Delta, where the region's best soils occur. A pipeline from the Panhandle could supplement this flow, providing some of the western settlements and people at Lake Ngami with water, and would have the least damaging effect on the Delta proper. At present the main argument against a pipeline is the expense of construction – in the region of ten times the cost of the proposed water project in the lower Delta. Although piped water is extremely expensive, this project should be economically feasible if the ultimate destination is the Orapa diamond mine. It may be the best long-term solution to the problem of how best to utilise the Delta's precious water resources.

Botswana's neighbour, Namibia, has already implemented the first stages of a water project, the Eastern National Water Carrier, which will take approximately two per cent of the Okavango's flow at the point where the river traverses the border between the two countries. It only remains for the final phase – the linking of an open canal to a pipeline that will carry water from the Okavango River – to be put into effect. This small off-take should not adversely affect the Delta, but the project does bring to light the fact that water is often an international resource, and complex politics are associated with water utilisation.

There is talk of a South African project to channel water from the Zambezi River, just above the Victoria Falls, where a 1,000-kilometre aqueduct would take one per cent of the Zambezi's flow across Botswana to the industrial cities of South Africa. This could provide Botswana with water for irrigation, for towns and for Orapa diamond mine, and eliminate the need to extract water from the Okavango. However, a large aqueduct traversing the northern wilderness of the Kalahari would provide as lethal a barrier to the movements of animals as the fences to the south. Namibia's open canal has already been dubbed the 'killer canal' by conservationists because of the large number of wild animals that have fallen into it and have been unable to escape.

Botswana is currently examining the feasibility of extracting water from its northern river, the Chobe. This could supply Orapa as well as provide the more developed eastern regions of Botswana with water for irrigation. Schemes to exploit large rivers that drain to the sea have their advantages as they are more robust systems than the Okavango, which flows into the Kalahari supporting a fragile web of life on its journey. Whichever option is finally chosen will have a far-reaching effect on the environment, so it is essential not to compromise by choosing a scheme of water extraction that may provide a short-term saving, but which is ecologically unsound.

Although the extraction of water from the Okavango is the most topical and immediate threat to the Delta, there are other factors which people fear could affect the future of the system. For a long time the tsetse fly was the guardian of Botswana's northern waterways, since the fly carries a minute parasite (trypanosome) which causes a deadly disease in both people and livestock, but to which wild animals have a natural immunity. Historically, the presence of the fly discouraged people from settling in the area of the Delta with their livestock; but recent success at eliminating most of the tsetse has removed this natural check.

The great rinderpest outbreak at the turn of the century decimated so many animals, both wild and domestic, that the fly, deprived of food, retreated northwards; people with livestock then moved in and settled on the edges of the Delta, some penetrating as far as Chief's Island. The tsetse population recovered and within fifty years had once more reclaimed its former territory. The war against tsetse began in earnest. Early attempts at its control were particularly destructive; over a period of twenty years, some 50,000 animals were killed, because they provide tsetse flies with food. Vast areas were cleared of trees to deprive the tsetse fly of the bush cover it needs to survive. These drastic control methods had little impact on the fly population.

By the 1960s, advances had been made in the use of chemicals. Knapsack sprayers hiked through the woodlands, spraying the base of trees with the deadly insecticide Dieldrin. Like DDT this chemical remains active for many years, accumulating in the food chain, and is thus lethal to all forms of life in an insidious way. In spite of this, only a small fraction of the infected area was cleared of tsetses. Great progress in control was made with the development of aerial spraying, and especially the use of a chemical, Endosulphan, that breaks down in sunlight and air and does not accumulate in the food chain like Dieldrin and DDT. Endosulphan is toxic to fish, but a method of spraying the chemicals in a fine mist, first pioneered in East Africa, was introduced. This method is known as ultra-low volume spraying. The chemicals are dispersed in a fine mist spray that drifts through the air, with only fifty per cent actually reaching the ground. Spraying occurs in such low concentrations that there is only danger to fish if an area is over-dosed due to pilot error, or in areas where the water is very shallow. It is considered to be the safest method of tsetse control yet devised.

Spraying is cyclical to match the life cycle of the tsetse fly, and it is this that makes the spraying programmes more specific to the fly. The tsetse fly is unique in that the female produces only one young, which develops inside her rather than in an egg. For some reason pregnant females are particularly resistant to chemicals, so another rather less specific chemical, called Deltamethrin, has been added to Endosulphan to form a 'chemical cocktail', the long-term effect of which is still not known. Unfortunately, this chemical kills other insects as well. There is concern that spraying will also kill a weevil which is being used as a biological control of the water weed, salvinia. Salvinia has infested the water of the Linyanti and Kwando swamps. It is a native of South America, and has caused great troubles in African waterways since there is no naturally occurring organism in Africa that controls it. A salvinia weevil, which has been found to check the weed's growth in Brazil, has been introduced, and appears to be gradually checking the growth of the weed in Botswana. The spread of salvinia into the Delta is greatly feared, as it will quickly spread through the waterways, blocking drainage lines, upsetting natural flow patterns, hindering access, and killing aquatic life. At present, salvinia is confined to the northern border rivers. A small outbreak in the southern Okavango Delta in 1986 was quickly controlled by the Aquatic Weeds Control Unit, which blocked off the infected lagoon and pumped it dry. There will, however, be a constant battle to prevent the salvinia weed from being brought into the Delta by the movement of boats and people.

In the last decade attempts have been made at widespread eradication of the tsetse fly, with the argument that it is less environmentally damaging to eliminate the fly, only spraying occasional outbreaks, than to spray the Delta repeatedly, year after year, as a means of control. Tsetse has now been virtually eliminated from the Okavango Delta. This is an achievement for the government, since the north of the country has been rid of a pest which brought death and suffering to its people, loss of livestock production, and a threat and nuisance to visitors.

However, many people fear that there is now a real threat that, in the absence of the tsetse fly, cattle will enter this wilderness for food and water. In fact the Delta is not good cattle country; it is temptingly lush, but the floodplain grasses are not as 'sweet' as those of the Kalahari sandveldt. Although many different species live in the Delta, the soils are essentially Kalahari sand and the system is too infertile to support very large numbers of animals. Most of the Delta's larger animals disperse into the Kalahari interior for better grazing as soon as the rains permit. These arguments may not deter the subsistence farmer, looking for grazing for his cattle, who sees these vast expanses of green grass. But the Buffalo Fence provides a physical barrier around part of the Delta, and it is there for a reason – to separate cattle from buffalo which carry the dreaded foot-and-mouth disease. An outbreak of foot-and-mouth could cripple Botswana's beef export market, so it is unlikely that cattle owners would be allowed to let their cattle cross the fence and risk infection. Indeed, the Delta has been designated a cattle-free zone and a comprehensive land use plan is currently being drawn up, designating areas for tourism, hunting, wildlife management, subsistence tribal areas and protected land. Hopefully, as we move towards the twenty-first century, sensible land control by man can take over from a biting fly in being the guardian of the wild.

How important is it that the Okavango should survive? There appears to be no argument that the Delta is a valuable and unique area to Botswana and to the world. The Okavango Delta and its associated areas provide a sanctuary to many rare and endangered animals, such as cheetahs, leopards, wild dogs and brown hyaenas. It is one of the most important wetlands in Africa, providing a breeding area for many rare birds such as wattled cranes, slaty egrets and pink-backed pelicans: the Panhandle is one of only three breeding areas in southern Africa for pink-backed pelicans, while the Delta is the only area in the world where the slaty egret breeds. The area attracts visitors from all over the world, who come to enjoy the wilderness and to see these rare creatures. Thus tourism is becoming one of Botswana's largest income earners, and in the north it provides more work than any other economic sector.

The swamp is a stable ecological system, more efficient at utilising nutrients and conserving water than any alternative system man could attempt to create. The Delta provides the livelihood of many people scattered around its edges, through hunting, fishing, and flood irrigation. More than half of Ngamiland's cattle depend on the Okavango for water. The Okavango is Botswana's water heritage, a resource more precious even than diamonds. Indeed, without it the country's largest diamond mine would cease production as soon as its groundwaters dry up. The way in which the Okavango Delta is utilised is of critical importance, for it is a fragile system and interference by man could damage and change it for ever. Beneath the shallow water lies Kalahari sand, ready to be burnt by the sun and blown away by the wind should that protective cloak of water disappear.

The Okavango Delta is internationally recognised as a unique ecological system. The International Union for the Conservation of Nature (IUCN) has supported the nomination of the Okavango as a World Heritage Site; there are ninety-one countries as signatories of the World Heritage Convention. In an analysis of the importance of the world's wilderness areas, the World Wildlife Fund (WWF) attached crucial importance to conserving the Okavango Delta for its uniqueness and diversity of natural life. They have urged Botswana to join both the World Heritage Convention and one of the world's oldest international conservation treaties, the Ramsar Convention, which was drawn up in 1971 and exists to protect the world's wetlands. The treaty is unique in its aim to conserve a single type of ecosystem. If the world considers the Okavango a unique and beautiful wilderness, it must contribute to its protection. By joining these treaties the Botswana government could benefit from worldwide recognition, advice and protection over international water disputes, and financial assistance for projects which might be more expensive than other alternatives, but better for the environment.

Nevertheless the Botswana government has already shown considerable commitment to protecting its natural resources, and is at present drawing up countrywide land-use plans, and developing a national conservation strategy. Addressing a public symposium on the Okavango Delta the President of Botswana, Dr Quett Masire, said, 'The Kalahari, semi-arid and without streams and rivers, is very different from the Okavango Delta. Yet both are valuable natural resources and both can be sensitive to misuse. Both could be destroyed through ignorance, haste or greed. It is our privilege to use them, but it is our duty to conserve them for the future.'

ACKNOWLEDGEMENTS

This book was produced at the same time as a series of three films on the ecology of northern Botswana. Both films and book are the result of team work and the assistance of innumerable people whom I would like to acknowledge here – my apologies to any I have inadvertently omitted.

This ambitious project, covering a vast area and complex subject, owes its existence to Michael Rosenberg of Partridge Films, who created and produced the films. I would like to thank him for giving me the opportunity to write this book. The films were made for the BBC series *The Natural World*.

The research, film footage and photographs are the result of nearly two years spent in the field in Botswana, and I would like to acknowledge the 'team' for their work: photographers Richard Foster, Jim Clare, Arthur Clare and Dereck Joubert, who shot the spectacular footage, together with their assistants and field researchers, Teresa Townsend, Carol Farneti and Beverly Joubert. Ken Oake and Tim Liversedge shot additional footage for the films, and the latter supplied photos for the book. I would like to thank the photographers, in particular Carol Farneti, whose beautiful photos illustrate the book. The base camp was managed by Sande Greer, and we would like to thank Lesego Tikologo, Christopher Hatsche, Steve Clarc, Babine Swanka, Boitimelo Mpho, Emerita Corey and Phodiso Seloilwe who looked after us and the camps at various stages throughout the project. David and Tessa Hartley kindly 'hosted' our camp on the remote island of Xugana in the Okavango Delta, and Ken and Mel Oake did likewise in Maun, assisted by their children Shareen and Hayden.

People in Botswana were generous with their help, many experts parting freely with their knowledge of the area – sometimes a lifetime's work. I would like to acknowledge the assistance of Pete Smith, Larry Patterson, Eleanor Warr, Festus Mugae, Charles Tiboni, Paul Schaller, Stewart Child, Nigel Hunter, Louis Nchindo, Seeiso Leephuko, Glenn Merron, Ron Auerbach, Mark Murray, David Parry, Allan Wellwood, Jeff Bowles, Wolf Haacke, Doug Williamson, Karen and Fred Ellery, John Benn, Alec Campbell, John Cooke, Paul Shaw and Richard Hartland-Rowe. On field trips we were assisted by Keith and Maggie Poppleton, Mike Slowgrove,

Jim Denbow, Richard Lee, George Calef, Neville Peake, Sam Miller, Carol and Camm Hughes, Nigel and Liz Ashby and Jack, Nikki and Ralph Bousfield. Tim and Bryony Longdon, Lee Ouzman and Mike van Ginkel kindly helped us get to the many remote places we visited. For their hospitality I would like to thank Judy Bowles, Eleanor Warr, June Liversedge, Mel Oake, June and Charlie Raitt, Mav and Dougald McDonald and Pam Ross. The sometimes complex logistics of getting the film team where they wanted to go, and keeping us and our material in touch with Partridge Films, London, was made possible by the work of Penny Barrow, Jenni Brand, Matildah Bethia and Janis Mullan. In London, the films were edited by Joy Chamberlain, Dave Dickie and Chris Frazer, assisted by Michelle Baughaun, Mark Fletcher and Revel Fox. Jennie Muskett wrote the music. The London team assisted in all aspects of production, not least in making Partridge a wonderful place to work – our thanks to Vanessa Boeye, Helen Wolfson, Richelle Shaw, Gill Seels, Andrea Florence and Niki Rathbone.

The Schaller-Peterson family played an important part for me personally: Janet delivered our daughter Lena, and Paul's computer in Maun delivered the manuscript! The text of the book was greatly improved by the comments of Sande Greer, Pete Smith, Tim Liversedge and Finn Ross – my thanks to them. The book was published by BBC Books and I would like to acknowledge the editor Tony Kingsford, Elinor Bagenal and Sarah Hoggett for their patient help, and Linda Blakemore for the design of the book.

We would all like to thank the Botswana government for permission to work in their wonderful country, and the people of Botswana who extended their courtesy to us during the project.

My thanks to Hugo van Lawick for his help and encouragement over the years. Finally, my love and thanks to my husband, Sande Greer, whose love, help and support made this book possible for me.

PICTURE CREDITS

BIBLIOGRAPHY

GENERAL

Bannister, A. and Johnson, P., *Okavango – sea of land, land of water*, Cape Struick Publishers, Cape Town, 1977.

Broadley, D.G. and Cock, E.V., *Snakes of Zimbabwe*, Longman Zimbabwe (Pty), 1975.

Campbell, A.C., *The guide to Botswana*, Winchester Press, Gaborone, 1980.

Coates Palgrave, K. *The trees of southern Africa*, Cape Struick Publishers, Cape Town, 1977.

Fry, C.H., *The bee-eaters*, T. and A.D. Poyser Ltd, Calton, England, 1984.

Lee, R.B., *The Kung San – men, women and work in a foraging society*, Cambridge University Press, 1979.

Luard, N., *The last wilderness: a journey across the great Kalahari desert*, Elm Tree Books/ Hamish Hamilton, London, 1981.

Miller, P. *Myths and legends of southern Africa*, T.V. Bulpin Publications (Pty) Ltd, Cape Town, 1979.

Owens, M. and D., *Cry of the Kalahari*, Collins, London, 1985.

Roberts, A., *The birds of South Africa*. Revised edition by McLachlan and Liversidge, London.

Shostak, M., *Nisa: the life and words of a !Kung woman*, Penguin, Harmondsworth, 1983.

Sillery, A., *Botswana: a short political history*, Methuen, London, 1974.

Skaife, S.H. *African insect life*, Cape Struick Publishers, Cape Town, 1979.

Styen, P., *Birds of prey of southern Africa*, David Philip Publications, Cape Town, 1982.

Van der Post, Laurens, *The lost world of the Kalahari*, Penguin, Harmondsworth, 1962.

SPECIALIST

Blomberg, G.E.D. 'Feeding and nesting ecology and habitat preferences of Okavango crocodiles', *Proceedings of the symposium on the Okavango Delta and its future utilisation*, Botswana Society, Gaborone (1976).

Bowles, J. 'Current activities in tsetse control in Botswana', *Kalahari Conservation Society Newsletter* 4 (1984), 1–12.

Brown, L.H. and Seely, M. 'Abundance of the pygmy goose *Nettapus auritus* in the Okavango swamps, Botswana', *Ostrich* 44 (1973), 94.

Bruton, M. and Merron, G. 'The Okavango Delta – give credit where credit is due', *African Wildlife* 39:2 (1985), 59–63.

Calef, G. 'Mapping the movements of Botswana's elephants', *Kalahari Conservation Society Newsletter* 16 (1987).

Campbell, A.C. 'Comment on Kalahari wildlife and the Kuke Fence', *Botswana Notes and Records* 13 (1981), 111–18.

Carter, J.M. 'The development of wildlife management areas in Botswana', *Which way Botswana's wildlife?* (Proceedings of the symposium of the Kalahari Conversation Society, Gaborone, Botswana, 1983), 63–73.

Child, G. 'The future of wildlife and rural land use in Botswana', *Proceedings, SARCCUS symposium on nature conservation as a form of land use*, Gorongosa National Park, Mozambique (1971), 78.

Child, G. 'Wildlife utilisation and management in Botswana', *Biol. Conserv.* 3 (1970), 18–22.

Collar, N.J. and Stuart, S.N. *Threatened birds of Africa and related islands: the ICBP/IUCN red data book* (part one), Cambridge, 1985.

CNPPA *The world's greatest natural areas: an indicative inventory of natural sites of World Heritage quality*, Eland, Switzerland: International Union for Conservation of Nature and Natural Resources (Commission on National Parks and Protected Areas), (1982).

Comrie-Greig, J. 'The Eastern National Water Carrier – "killer canal" or life-giving artery? Or both?' *African Wildlife* 40 (1986), 68–73.

Cooke, H.J. 'The Kalahari today: a case of conflict over resource use', *The Geographical Magazine* 151:1 (1985), 75–85.

Cooke, H.J. 'The origin of the Makgadikgadi Pans', *Botswana Notes and Records* 11 (1979), 37–42.

Cooke, H.J. 'The struggle against environmental degradation – Botswana's experience', *Desertificational Control*, UNEP, 8 (1983), 12.

Davies, J.E. *The history of tsetse fly control in Botswana*, Government of Botswana Department of Tsetse Fly Control, Gaborone, 1981.

Denbow, J.R. 'Early Iron Age remains from the Tsodilo Hills, north-western Botswana', *South African Journal of Science* 76:10 (1980), 474–75.

Douthwaite, R.J., Fox, P.J., Matthieson, P., and Russell-Smith, A. *The environmental impact of aerosols of Endosulfan applied to tsetse fly control in the Okavango Delta, Botswana*. Final report of the Endosulfan Monitoring Project, Overseas Development Administration, London (1981).

Du Toit, A.L. In *The geology of South Africa*, edited by Haughton, S.H. London: Oliver and Boyd, 1954.

Fowkes, J.D. *The contribution of the tourist industry to the economy of Botswana*. Report to the Kalahari Conservation Society, Gaborone, Botswana, Feb. 1985.

Games, I. 'Feeding and movement patterns of the Okavango sitatunga', *Botswana Notes and Records* 16 (1984), 131–37.

Grove, A.T. 'Landforms and climatic change in the Kalahari', *The Geographic Journal* 135 (1969), 191.

Haacke, W.D. 'The herpetology of the southern Kalahari domain', *Proceedings of the symposium of the Kalahari ecosystem* (ed. de Graafe, G. and van Rensburg, D.J.), Pretoria (1984), 117–86.

Hartland-Rowe, R. 'The adaptive value of synchronous emergence in the tropical African mayfly (*Povilla adusta*): a preliminary investigation, *Proceedings of the fourth international conference on Ephemeroptera* (ed. V. Landan et al.), 1984, 283–89.

Hedger, R.S. 'Foot-and-mouth disease in wildlife with particular reference to the African buffalo', *Wildlife Diseases* (1976), 235–43.

Huey, R.B. and Pianka, E.R. 'Natural selection for juvenile lizards mimicking noxious beetles', *Science* 195 (1977), 201–203.

Kalahari Conservation Society (1986a) Southern Okavango Integrated Water Development Project, *Kalahari Conservation Society Newsletter* 11:8.

Kingdon, J. *East African mammals – an atlas of evolution in Africa*, vols I–VII, London, Academic Press, 1974.

Leistner, O.A. *The plant ecology of the southern Kalahari*, Government of South Africa, Department of Agricultural Services, Botanical Memoir no. 38, Pretoria (1967).

Liversedge, T.N. 'A study of Pel's fishing owl, *Scotopelia peli Bonaparte 1850*, in the Panhandle region of the Okavango Delta, Botswana', *Proceedings of the fourth Pan-African ornithological Congress* (1980): 291–99.

Louw, G. and Seely, M. *Ecology of Desert Organisms*, New York: Longman, 1982.

Loveridge, J.P. 'Strategies of water conservation in southern African frogs', *Zoologica Africana* 11:2 (1976), 319–33.

McCarthy, J., Ellery, W., Rogers, K., Cairncross, M. and Ellery, K. 'The roles of sedimentation and plant growth in changing flow patterns in the Okavango, Botswana', *South African Journal of Science*, 83, 579–584.

Maclean, G.L. 'Arid-zone adaptations in southern African birds', *Cimbebesia*, series A, 2:15 (March 1974), 163–76.

Masire, Q.K.J. Opening speech, *Proceedings of the symposium on the Okavango Delta and its future utilisation*, Botswana Society, Gaborone, 1976.

Meeuse, C. 'The pollination biology of *Nympheae*', *Proceedings of the second international congress of systematic and evolutionary biology*, University of British Columbia, Vancouver (1980).

Merron, G. 'Fish research in the Okavango Delta', *Kalahari Conservation Society Newsletter* 11:9 (1986).

Nchunga, M.L. 'The future of parks and reserves', *Which way Botswana's wildlife?* (Proceedings of the symposium of the Kalahari Conservation Society, Gaborone, Botswana, 1983), 75–79.

Nel, J.A. and Bester, M.H. 'Communication

in the southern bat-eared fox, *Otocyon m. megalotis*', Z. Saugetierkunde 48 (1983), 277–90.

Newlands, G. *Biogeography and ecology of southern Africa*, ed. Werger, M.J.A., The Hague: Dr W. Junk, 1978.

Ngwamatsoko, K.T. 'Lessons for future livestock development projects in Botswana: wildlife resources considerations', *Proceedings of the symposium on Botswana's first Livestock Development Project and its future implications*, National Institute of Research, Gaborone, Botswana, June 1982, 143–63.

Parris, R. 'The important role of Kalahari Pans', *African Wildlife* 24 (1970), 234–37.

Paterson, L. 'An introduction to the ecology and zoo-geography of the Okavango Delta', *Proceedings of the symposium on the Okavango Delta and its future utilisation*, Botswana Society, Gaborone (1976), 55–60.

Potten, D.H. 'Aspects of the recent history of Ngamiland', *Botswana Notes and Records* 8 (1974), 63–86.

Report of the UNEP clearing-house technical mission to Botswana, UNEP, Nairobi (1983).

Republic of Botswana, *National Development Plan 1985–91*, Gaborone: Ministry of Finance and Development Planning, 1985.

Roostee, R. 'Molapo farming in environmental conservation and ecological principles for economic development', *Proceedings of seminar on environmental conservation and ecological principles for economic development*, Maun, Botswana: Department of Wildlife and National Parks (1982).

Shaw, P.A. 'A historical note on the outflows of the Okavango Delta system', *Botswana Notes and Records* 16 (1984), 128.

Shaw, P.A. 'The desiccation of Lake Ngami: a historical perspective', *The Geographical Journal* 151:3.

Silberbauer, G.B. *Report to the Bechuanaland government on the Bushman survey*, Government of Botswana (1965), 56–8.

Smith, P. '*Salvinia molesta:* an alien water weed in Botswana', *Kalahari Conservation Society Newsletter* 7 (1985), 10–12.

Smith, P.A. 'An outline of the vegetation of the Okavango drainage system', *Proceedings of*

the symposium on the Okavango and its future utilisation, Botswana Society, Gaborone (1976), 93–112.

Taylor, C.R. 'The eland and the oryx', *Scientific American*, 220:1 (Jan. 1969).

Thompson, K. 'Ecology, management and utilisation of aquatic and semi-aquatic vegetation in the Okavango Delta, Botswana', *Technical report for UNDP project BOT/506*, UN/FAO Land and Water Development Division (1974).

Tinley, K.L. *An ecological reconnaisance of the Moremi Wildlife Reserve, Botswana*, Johannesburg: Okavango Wildlife Society, 1966.

Tlou, T. *A history of Ngamiland – 1750 to 1906 – the formation of an African state*, Macmillan, Botswana, 1985.

Tlou, T. 'The taming of the Okavango swamps – the utilisation of a riverine environment, 1750–1800', *Botswana Notes and Records* 6 (1972), 147–50.

United Nations, *Investigation of the Okavango Delta as a primary water resource for Botswana*, UNDP/FAO, Gaborone, Botswana, AG:DP/BOT/71/506, Technical report, vol. II, 1977.

Van Voorthuizen, E.G. 'The mopane tree', *Botswana Notes and Records*, 8 (1974), 227–30.

Veenendaal, E.M. and Opschoor, J.B. 'Botswana's beef exports to the EEC: economic development at the expense of a deteriorating environment', Institute of Environmental Studies, Free University, Amsterdam, 1985, typescript p. 46.

Welcomme, R.L. 'The role of African flood-plains in fisheries', ed. M. Smart *International conference on the conservation of wetlands and waterfowl, Heiligenhafen, F.R. Germany, Dec. 1974*, Slimbridge U.K.: International Wildfowl Research (1976).

Williamson, D.T. and Williamson, J.E. 'Kalahari ungulate movement study', *Final report to Frankfurt Zoological Society and World Wildlife Fund* (1985), pp. 123 ff.

Wilson, B.H. 'Some natural and man-made changes in the channels of the Okavango Delta', *Botswana Notes and Records* 15 (1983), 138.

INDEX AND SPECIES LIST